IN SEARCH OF
WELSH ANCESTRY

Uncle Emrys worked all this out ages ago.

IN SEARCH OF WELSH ANCESTRY

Gerald Hamilton-Edwards

GENEALOGICAL PUBLISHING CO., INC.
Baltimore 1986

Published in the U.S.A. by
Genealogical Publishing Co., Inc.
Baltimore, Maryland, 1986

Library of Congress Catalogue Card Number 85-70028
International Standard Book Number 0-8063-1122-3

Published in Great Britain, 1986, by
Phillimore & Co., Ltd.
Shopwyke Hall, Chichester, Sussex

Printed and bound in Great Britain

Dedicated to
Adelaide Ross (née Phillpotts)
whose kind encouragement of my writing
has been such a beneficial incentive to me

CONTENTS

Appendices

LIST OF TEXT ILLUSTRATIONS

ACKNOWLEDGEMENTS

I owe much gratitude to the Librarian and staff of the National Library of Wales for their assistance in many directions in writing this book. In particular my thanks go to Mr. R. McDonald, Assistant Keeper, Department of MSS and Records, for his letters giving me considerable information of his department and to Mrs. Nan Jenkins of the Department of Printed Books giving me information of books and articles on Welsh names.

I am also particularly appreciative of the trouble Mr. D. Williams has taken in selecting a suitable will and inventory of the 17th century as an illustration for this book and also for giving me information on certain words and expressions in the will in question.

I am also indebted to Mr. Whittow of Hindhead, Surrey for supplying me with pedigrees of the Whittow family of Pembrokeshire, which I have been able to incorporate mainly in the pedigree of the Whittows of Pembrokeshire used in this work, and to Mr. Mark Whittow, Research Fellow of Oriel College, Oxford, for putting me in touch with his cousin regarding this pedigree.

I am once again grateful to Joan Harris of Crownhill, Plymouth for her line illustrations, some of which have been used in my earlier books. I also appreciate the help I have had from Stephan Natynczuk in compiling the index. I am also indebted for help in checking the index to Colin Harris of the Bodleian Library and to Mrs. Eileen Ridley of Northway, Oxford.

INTRODUCTION

AN OUTLINE OF WELSH HISTORY

THE NAME WALES, given by the English to the territories in the west of the country, meant 'The land of the Foreigner'.

Christianity survived in this western part, and between the years 500 and 560 the bishoprics of Llandaff, Bangor, St David and Asaph were all founded. There were differences in the formation of the Celtic from the Roman church, and after St Augustine landed in AD 603 the Welsh bishops talked with him to see whether they could show a re-united front in evangelising the Saxons, but they failed to come to any agreement. Wales, therefore, remained isolated in its Christianity from the rest of the kingdom.

That period from AD 500 to the time of William the Conqueror was a disturbed period for Wales. The death of Cadwallader, which was about AD 664, ended the contest between the Angles and Britain for supremacy. It was only the central district of Wales, roughly the modern Wales, which retained independence, and was governed by a number of petty princes.

Not until Offa of Mercia (757–796) did the conquest of Wales really begin. During the war against them Offa extended the frontier west of the Severn, so as to include Shrewsbury, and, in order to substantiate his conquest, he made a dyke from the Wye to the Dee, which has become known as Offa's Dyke.

During the time of Edward the Elder and Athelstan the wars with the Welsh continued, and this resulted in the overlordship of the English king never being really substantiated, and when Canute became king he had to march into Wales once again to subdue a rising there.

Trouble broke out again in the time of King Harold, who led his forces into Wales and defeated the Welsh prince, establishing his supremacy, and was acknowledged as king by the Welsh. This was, of course, the King Harold who was killed by an arrow at the Battle of Hastings.

William the Conqueror never really succeeded in conquering Wales and the Welsh princes. His position was very insecure and he set up the three earls of Chester, Shrewsbury and Hereford to stand guard along the Welsh frontier, along which there was constant border trouble. William II promised to give land to those of his barons who should be successful in attacking the Welsh. The land which was conquered by them was maintained by a succession of Norman castles, which resulted in Wales being finally subdued.

In Henry I's reign he made settlements of Flemings in Pembrokeshire, partly for the purpose of subduing and civilising the Welsh people. It would seem that about the year 1106, a year of great storms in Flanders, the coast of that country was in many places carried away and the sea inundated huge tracts of the country. As a result a great body of the Flemish sought asylum in England, where they were received kindly by Henry, and then they dispersed themselves among the different counties. However this did not work very satisfactorily and Henry decided to remove them to the district of Roos in Pembrokeshire to the westward of the town of Haverfordwest, a place where a strong castle was built.

Later a second inundation in Flanders about the year 1113 sent another body of refugees to England and Henry, anxious also to subdue the rising power of Gruffydd ab Rhys (d. 1137) in South Wales, settled this colony also in this part of Pembrokeshire and told his commanders in that part to provide some form of habitation and means of subsistence for them, on condition that they should consider themselves his subjects and be obedient to his officers. He is also believed to have placed English settlers amongst them to teach them the English language and inculcate in them English customs.

So Pembrokeshire became known as 'Little England' and descendants of both the Flemish and English settlers there have remained to the present day in the southern parts of that county.

The pedigree of the Whittow family shown in this book does not go back further than about 1700. This is due mainly to the fact that the parish registers of Pembrokeshire do not extend back further than about that date, but it is considerably probable that the ancestors of this family were Flemish immigrants to this part of the country.

Another factor in Pembrokeshire history is that Gilbert Strongbow managed to recover much of his territories in Cardiganshire which he had lost previously. However, Rhys ab Gruffydd, Prince of South Wales (d. 1197, son of the above Gruffydd ab Rhys), angered by the repeated injuries by the English to his people, was making constant attacks and inroads to the homes of the Flemings, ravaging their country. A few years later he repeated his attacks and took and destroyed the castle of Kilgerran as a pledge of his strength and importance.

The 12th century saw a revival of Welsh power, during which time Owen, King of North Wales, successfully resisted Henry II. Then, in the reign of King John, Llewelyn ap Jorwerth attained such power that the English king tried to obtain his submission by giving his daughter Johanna to him in marriage. But even under those circumstances in 1210 John found himself compelled to make war against this rebellious son-in-law. Llewelyn and his barons seized Shrewsbury and then drove out the English garrison at Caermarthen and Cardigan.

Later his grandson, Llewelyn ap Gruffydd (1246–83), attained great power, siding with the barons in their war with Henry III, eventually being acknowledged as Prince of Wales. When Edward I came to the throne, Llewelyn refused to do homage to him, and this led to the expedition of that monarch into Wales and the final conquest of the principality.

Following this, Wales went through an unhappy period. Disorders and rebellions prevailed and led in 1478 to the establishment of the Council of Wales and the Marches, which Henry VII later made a permanent council. Owen Glendower was leader of the rebellions of this period.

However, the advent of Henry VII to the English throne, after his successful defeat of Richard III at the Battle of Bosworth, introduced into Welsh history a happy period. Henry VII was born in Pembroke Castle and was partly Welsh, and his son Henry VIII determined on a new settlement for the principality. Professor David Williams in his *History of Modern Wales* recounts [p. 34] that in Edward, Lord Herbert of Cherbury's *Life of Henry VIII* is preserved a petition from Wales 'craving to be received and adopted into the same laws and privileges which your other subjects enjoy' and, with some apology that in the past the Welsh had supported the House of York, 'the petitioners protested their unfailing loyalty thereafter to the Tudors'. They asked for union as a reward for this loyalty. That the Welsh spoke a different language, they claimed, should be no bar. 'Your Highness', they said, 'will have but the more tongues to serve you.'

Parliamentary representation was given to Wales in 1535 and in 1542 the King's Courts superseded the old jurisdiction of the Lords Marchers. At this time the counties of Denbigh, Montgomery, Monmouth, Brecon and Radnor were formed.

During the Civil War Wales favoured Charles I and during the 18th century the Welsh were much influenced by the Methodist revival under Howell Harris and Rowlands. The rise of Nonconformity in Wales and the Welsh Calvinists will be described in a later chapter.

The Union of England and Wales was completed in 1830, when the special judicial system, which had continued until then, was abolished and the legal system became similar to that of England.

The 19th century was also a time of great advances in education, and Wales was given its separate Church on the disestablishment of the English Church in Wales. Another event of that time was the discovery of mineral wealth in the Principality.

The idea of a National University for Wales had been mooted at the beginning of the century. In 1853 it was revived and shortly after that university colleges were established at Aberystwyth, Cardiff and Bangor, to be followed in 1893 by the charter of the University of Wales.

Welsh is still spoken in the more rural parts.

Chapter One

INFORMATION FROM RELATIVES

BEFORE YOU SPEND any time doing research you should certainly find out whether any earlier work has been done on the family. It is very annoying to spend much time finding out about the family only to discover after a great deal of work that 'Great Uncle Owen did all that years ago'. So do make sure that the family has not been investigated earlier: if it has, you may be able to add something to the discoveries made at that time. If nothing has been done, then your first step is to find out what you can from relatives in the family, particularly those of earlier generations. Depending on your own age, both your parents may be alive or even your grandparents or great-uncles and great-aunts, and they may be able to tell you a great deal which will save much research.

Sometimes it is a maiden aunt or great-aunt who has taken an interest in the family. This may be because, not having made any additions to the branches of the family, she is particularly interested in its roots. Very often there is one person in the family in each generation who has taken some interest in it. Sometimes they are at first rather reluctant to talk about it, but you must persist, pointing out to them that you are determined to investigate the family and that, the more they can tell you about it, the more money you will be able to save in obtaining certificates and other material which may not then be necessary.

It is a good idea, really, to send out a pro-forma to the members of the family, particularly the older generation. At the end of this book, as an appendix, there is a suggested pro-forma that you should use. Make sure you leave plenty of room for people's replies. You can get the pro-forma xeroxed or reproduced by some other method in sufficient quantities for the numbers you are likely to need. By doing so you will show members to whom it is sent that you are in earnest in your research, and by sending them a form you give them time to think about the answers before sending them back to you. Some of them, of course, may ignore it completely, or say they know nothing about it at all. Nevertheless it will stimulate some interest in the family history and cause the various members of it to talk about it, and when the replies are put together they may reveal a considerable amount of information. Anyway, from the return of these forms you will be able to build up some kind of picture of the background of the family.

You may notice that members of the family to whom you later talk begin by saying they know nothing about it, but in the end it turns out that they know a considerable amount. Welsh people are proud of their ancestry and very often there are traditions which have survived in the family; although they may have been exaggerated in the course of time, nevertheless they have a basis of truth in them. You should always, therefore, follow up any of these traditions. Some of them may be exaggerated and rather pretentious. Families sometimes have a story that they should have been entitled to some money in Chancery which they could not claim because they had not sufficient money themselves to fight the case, or perhaps there is some rumour of a right to a particular estate or title. These kinds of remembrances are usually just pipe-dreams. So many families like to feel that they came from a rather aristocratic or wealthy background. But the family historian must be a searcher after truth and truth alone. Your pro-forma will enquire about any deeds or documents affecting the family which have survived, and you should try to get these collected in or at any rate seek to be allowed to make copies of them. Naturally originals or copies of wills, marriage-settlements, deeds of family arrangements, births, baptisms, marriages, death and burial certificates are all of great value and the more of these you can discover the less you will need to spend money in obtaining certificates from the civil registration. Also graves and their upkeep; you may come across some receipt for the upkeep of a grave somewhere and this will give you an idea where the family lived.

If you are particularly lucky you may find someone has an old family bible in which, because it used to be the custom, are entered baptisms, marriages and burials on the leaves provided in these family bibles for this purpose, and you may obtain much information from this source. Such family bibles are particularly valuable if they go back earlier than Civil Registration, which in England and Wales began in July 1837.

But even the later entries are useful because they give you the dates and, though you may still find it necessary to obtain civil registrations, this source will tell you the date of the event and therefore save you going through volumes of indexes. The Welsh nation has been a closely-knit race, proud of their families and their ancestry. The saying 'as long as a Welsh pedigree' is indicative of this.

Perhaps one of the fascinations in tracing your families is the great variety of events in which you will find they were concerned, because no family history is exactly similar to another family history. Naturally if a person was high up in the social structure of the country, he or she will be easier to trace than those in more humble circumstances. This is particularly true of people who owned land and may have held it for generations. For one thing, they are people who would have stayed some time in one place and, secondly, they would probably have been of some local importance and be people who would have made wills, which one should be able to trace. This of course is true, but the majority of people would not have come from upper class families, who are necessarily a minority.

But do not let this depress you, because the history of people farther down the social scale can be just as interesting as those higher up. It is always exciting to discover in what sort of way your ancestors earned their living, and when you find they were in some particular trade or occupation you will then get interested in what that occupation or trade required them to do and know. This also gives greater interest to your family story.

The existence and survival of various records is naturally a factor which affects your search. If you come from a family which lived on one of the islands off Pembrokeshire which was not careful in keeping its parish registers, and did not keep them from an early period, then your task would be increased and more difficult.

Another matter which affects your work is the surname. If it is a very uncommon surname it will be easier to trace than a common one. One of the difficulties about tracing in Welsh sources is that the number of surnames, when surnames were adopted there, is comparatively small, which means that a great number of people held and hold the same surname. This led to various nicknames being given to them regarding the type of trade they were doing, such as 'Thomas the Milk' or 'Robert the Meat', and sometimes different names have been added, which may be either from the female side or perhaps from some place. You will find more about that in the next chapter on Welsh Christian and surnames.

Even when the surname is a common one there are various factors which are helpful. No doubt one of the most important of these is the conservative attitude to Christian names which most nations, and certainly the Welsh, possessed. Where the eldest son may be named after the father or after the paternal grandfather, the second son might have a name from the mother's father or else some other name that had existed in the family for some time. In fact you will find Christian names occurring again and again as you uncover each generation, and, if you find some Christian name coming into the family which you have never come across before, then you may perhaps query whether this person is a relation or not. Quite possibly the name came in through somebody on the mother's side, or else possibly from some influential godfather or godmother. But certainly, when you get back to about the middle of the 19th century, you may be fairly sure that the child was named after someone of an earlier generation.

If an unusual Christian name was in use in the family this can be a valuable clue. Donald Steel, the well-known genealogical writer, has made some research into Christian names, although, as he has said himself, a great deal more research could be done in this field. There is an article by him on the descent of Christian names in the June 1962 issue of *The Genealogists' Magazine*. There are various families where an unusual Christian name has continued for some generations and this has been a valuable link in tracing the family. The name of Rydian, for instance, has been maintained in the family of the Marquess of Bute and this is a Welsh name, but in quite ordinary families you may find the same continuance of a particular Christian name. Also, surnames which later were used as Christian names can be very indicative of some connection with that family, though it may only indicate a godfather or a particular patron of the family which caused it to be adopted.

Another important factor is the way in which families continued in the same trade for generations, and this can be helpful. They may, for instance, have been apprenticed in this trade and the Society of Genealogists, for the period from 1710 to 1760, has an index of apprentices at a time when there was a tax on apprenticeship, and this nearly always gives the name of one parent, usually the father, and the name of the person to whom they were apprenticed. Then again another factor is that the family remained in one particular area. If they remained in the same parish you may be able to trace the family back in that parish as far back as the register itself stretches. However, you must be very wary of this because, although people sometimes imagine that, if you find them by the 18th century in one parish, they probably have been in that parish for generations, this was not by any means always the case. Mobility was greater in the past than people sometimes imagine. They may not have moved far but on the other hand they could quite easily move thirty or forty miles to a different parish, perhaps because of their marriage, and you may have to search around an area in the county. Another reason why people sometimes moved was because they were employed by a certain squire in their own area who also owned property in other parts of the country and sometimes, if in one part he was not doing too well, he might offer his employees employment on another of his estates elsewhere. It is therefore a good thing to find out something about the local landowner, who probably employed many of the people there, as to where, for instance, he had other property, if you find the family disappearing suddenly from the parish.

You need also to make sure that the particular family you are tracing has not appeared in print in one of the many volumes that have been produced giving accounts of families. In this respect T. R. Thomson's *Catalogue of British Family History* is a valuable book and the Society of Genealogists has a copy of the last edition with some manyscript additions to it. The *British Catalogue of Printed Books* is a useful source, because family histories are listed under each surname at the beginning of that name. You can also discover any recent publication of family histories from the *British National Bibliography*, and these appear under classification No. 929. You can find this in any large library and certainly in the National Library of Wales, if you yourself are living in Wales. A number of printed family histories have appeared in the various publications of *Landed Gentry*. This work has been published since 1840 and there are numerous Welsh families within its covers, though there has never been a separate *Landed Gentry* for Wales, as there has been for Ireland.

Three other books are particularly useful: George Marshall's *Genealogist's Guide* (last edition 1903) with J. B. Whitmore's supplement to it called *A Genealogical Guide* (1947). These indicate 'any descent of three generations in male line which have been discovered in a wide range of publications'. There has been a further addition to this, bringing it up to date. Geoffrey B. Barrow's *Genealogist's Guide* (1977) brings Marshall and Whitmore up to 1976.

The possibility of your family having a rightful claim to armorial bearings may need investigating. There may well be rumours that you were entitled to a crest and arms, but unfortunately so many families, particularly in the 19th century, assumed they were entitled to certain arms of other families of the same surname as themselves, to which they were not in fact entitled. The only way to make sure of this is to apply to the College of Arms in London who will not charge a very large fee to investigate the possibility of your armigerous rights. There are also certain books on Welsh armigerous families which will be mentioned later.

From the time when you start searching you should aim at keeping your records in a systematic manner. In my general book *In Search of Ancestry* I have written a chapter on 'Keeping your records' which you might find worthwhile studying. Certainly you should get a filing cabinet and file your information on cards or slips of 8 in. x 6 in. and others of 3 in. x 5 in. in the way suggested, either keeping them in alphabetical order, or in some other classified order, according to circumstances, as you find convenient.

Also there are today various means of copying documents, which will help to keep your records. The Rank Xerox system, for instance, which quickly gives you an exact copy of the original. Most record offices today have means of copying documents and the National Library of Wales in particular has this facility. This allows you to examine documents at your leisure at home and be certain that you have not missed out any points, which is quite likely to happen if you merely make abstracts on the spot.

It is always useful to make a rough pedigree showing how far you have progressed, and a chart pedigree is one of the clearest ways of doing this and will help you with your further work. Once again the chapter in the above-mentioned book describes how you can do this by using either a dyeline or a xerox process of making copies of your pedigree, because if is always useful to be able to have other copies made which you can then show to or send out to other members of the family in the hope of getting their comments, and possibly corrections.

Letters of past members of the family.

Chapter Two

WELSH CHRISTIAN AND SURNAMES

IT WAS NOT until the 16th century that the Welsh people began to assume settled surnames. Before that they had used patronymics; that is to say, a person was described as 'John, son of Robert' or 'Richard, son of Owen'. The Welsh used the abbreviations 'ab' and 'ap' abbreviated from 'mab' and 'map' meaning 'son'. Usually it was sufficient to differentiate the various Johns, Owens and so forth by simply mentioning their fathers, or possibly their grandfather as well, such as 'John ab Owen ap Richard'. For this reason Christian names were important in the country. There were certain Christian names which, when surnames began to be taken, were most commonly taken as surnames, having been the father's Christian name. Thus 'Robert ap Richard' would be known as Robert Richard, and Richard would become the surname which would be handed down the generations to come.

There are certain Christian names which are Welsh. The majority of these are listed below. It is estimated that eight out of ten people in Wales, when they adopted a surname, took their father's name as their surname:

Alan, Allan, Allen, Alun	Gladys	Llew
Aneurin	Griffith, Gruffydd	Llewel(l)yn
Arianwen	Gwenfrew	Lloyd
Bettrys	Gwenhwyfar	Meredith
Boyd	Gwilym	Merlin
Bronwen	Gwladys	Morgan
C'nan	Gwyneth	Pugh
Dafod, Dafydd	Gwynne	Roy
Dai	Hew, Hu	Taffy
Deiniol	Hoel, Howell	Tafline
Deirdre	Idris	Trefor
Eiluned	Ifor	Tudor
Emlyn	Iolo	Vida
Emrys	Jenkin	Win
Evan	Kay	Winifred, Winifrid
Gawain, Gawaine, Gawen	Lewis	Winnie

Percy Hide Reaney, in his *Dictionary of British Surnames* (2nd edn. 1976) writes of Welsh names that, in 1292, 48 per cent. were patronymic. He goes on to state that it was only in the reign of Henry VIII that hereditary surnames began to be adopted among the gentry of Wales, and it was from them that the custom spread to ordinary people, but that even as late as the 19th century in country districts, mentioning particularly Merionethshire, it was still not uncommon for a man to refer to himself by a patronymic.

William Camden (1551–1623) the antiquary and historian, relates how in the time of King Henry VII 'an ancient worshipful gentleman of Wales, being called at the pannel of a Jurie by the name of "Thomas ap William ap Thomas ap Richard ap Hoel ap Euen-Veghan"' was advised by the Judge 'to leave that old manner' and take a surname. He acted on this advice and took his surname from his estate of Moston, which, in its modified form of 'Mostyn' became the surname of his descendants, and later the surname of the family holding both a barony and a baronetcy, which survive today.

The 'Worthy Juryman' in being called by his ancestors' names in this way was, as is seen, covering six generations. Allowing 30 years for a generation this means that his ancestors' names as called covered approximately 180 years. However, the information about his ancestors was merely nominal. You learn nothing of their occupation, of the period, or of dates when they were born, married or died, none of the wife's names and, from a family history point of view, it was interesting but not very informative. 'As long as a Welsh pedigree' is a well-known saying, but the family historian likes to know more than the mere Christian name of his ancestors.

While a number of names, as we have seen in the above list, were particularly Welsh, this does not mean that they were the most common names in use. The most common Christian names in Wales were John, William, David, Thomas and Evan. These names are reflected in the most common surnames, when these were adopted, namely Jones, Williams, Davies, Thomas and Evans. It will be noticed that the surname 'Smith', which is the most common surname in both England and Scotland, does not appear among these five most common surnames in Wales. Prys Morgan, in his chapter on Welsh surnames in his *Background to Wales: a course of studies in modern Welsh life* (1968) tells an amusing story illustrating how common the name 'Jones' is in Wales. One of the leaders of the Labour Party after leaving his train at Carmarthen, asked the taxi-driver to take him to 'Mr. Jones, the Agent'. The taxi-driver then enquired 'Well, it depends which you want, Mr. Jones the Liberal Agent, Mr. Jones the Tory Agent, Mr. Jones the Labour Agent, or Mr. Jones the Plad Cymru Agent'. John, in the Welsh language, has various equivalents: 'Sion', 'Ifan', 'Ieuan' or 'Iwan'.

If a son was named after his father in the days of patronymics, 'fychan', meaning 'junior', would be used: thus 'Sion fychan' meant 'John Junior', since his father was also named John, and this was the method by which he was differentiated from him.

Sometimes a boy might be given a nickname, such as 'Sion Gochy', if he was a redhead, but he would not regard this as a 'proper' name. If a young man's hair was grey coloured, he might keep the name of Lloyd. Surnames based on nicknames were less common than in England and Scotland. Sometimes the mother's name might be taken with the father's and mother's combined, such as Parry-Williams, or Lloyd-Jones.

Because so many Welsh surnames, when they were adopted, were the same, other means of identification, as mentioned, had to be taken. Sometimes people locally were given indications of their occupation, such as 'John the Milk' or 'William the Meat', but these were just local nicknames.

Quite likely, in your research for information from relatives, you will be told 'We always spelt the name with one "r"' or some other variation. Dr. P. H. Reaney, in his *Dictionary of British Surnames*, one of the greatest authorities on British surnames, has written 'The man who says his surname was always spelt as it is today is talking rank nonsense'. Anthony Camp, in *Everyone has Roots* (1978), gives us intriguing information on the variations and changes surnames have undergone during the centuries of their existence. Before about 1800 the majority of people were illiterate and even some squires were quite pleased with themselves if they were able to append their signature to some document. As a result most spelling was phonetic, as written down possibly by some parson or some clerk. He mentions the case of the Welshman who was designated 'affer david' whose name turned out to be the reading of the word 'affidavit'. He also mentions that 'Goulby is found to come from Goulsbra, Ivereigh from Ivory, and Kellet is found earlier as Qualet' and 'Hoyle' is a South Yorkshire pronunciation of 'Hole'. In my own family, my father's mother's family insisted that their name of Morison has always been spelt with one 'r' but I found, on researching the family, that of course the name was constantly spelt with two 'r's and with other variations. In fact they might earlier have been related to the Gilmours, since the Gallic name for Gilmore or Gilmour was Gille Moire, 'servant of (the Virgin) Mary' and its translation into English was Mary's servant, which in turn became Morison or Morrison, probably one serving in a church or chapel dedicated to the Virgin Mary. Thus Gilmore, Gilmour and Morison, Morrison, had the same derivation, one from the Gallic form, the other from the English form. You will realise, therefore, that before your surname came to you in its present form, it may have been through many changes.

When surnames were established the consonants in 'ab' or 'ap' were sometimes transferred to the beginning of the Christian name. Thus 'ab Evan' became 'Beavan', or 'Bevan'; 'ab Owein' became 'Bowen'; 'ab Robin' became 'Brobin', or 'Brobyn'. The 'p' in 'ap' was carried into several names; 'ap Harry' became 'Parry'; 'ap Howel' became 'Powell'; 'ap Richard', 'Pri(t)chard'; 'ap Robert', 'Probert'; 'ap Robin', 'Probin'; 'ap Hugh', 'Pugh'; and 'ap Humphrey', 'Pumphrey', or 'Pumfrey'.

Chapter Three

CIVIL REGISTRATIONS

WHEN ONCE YOU have collected the preliminary information from the family and other ready-made sources, you now have to start on your first practical adventure. The civil registration for Wales is the same as for England; in other words it is the civil registration for England and Wales. You naturally must use this civil registration as much as you possibly can. This goes back to July 1837 which may take you back, according to your own age, to your grandparents, great-grandparents or even possibly great-great-grandparents, and if you are fortunate in having a marriage just within the 1837 period, you then get the parentage of both the bride and bridegroom.

The registers for the whole of England and Wales are held at the General Register House, St Catherine's House, 100 Kingsway, London, WC2B 6JB, where there are general indexes in quarterly volumes in one alphabetical arrangement. The indexes for births and marriages are at St Catherine's House, but those for deaths are at Alexandra House, which is just across the road, almost opposite.

There are also district registers kept in the district registries of births, marriages and deaths in each locality. If you are absolutely certain that your ancestors came from an area within a district registry somewhere in Wales, it would be easier and quicker for you to search the local indexes, for these are far smaller and very often they have an index covering perhaps five years or even more in one alphabetical arrangement. Therefore, this should be far quicker for you because in one index you would cover perhaps five years but at St Catherine's House you would use 20 quarterly indexes to cover that number of years and one can imagine the difference in time this would take. But the main point is you must be reasonably certain that your ancestor or ancestors were born in the area of this district registry and if there was any doubt about it you might find you yourself would have to go to London or get someone to search for you at the General Register Office.

You can find out where the local district register is and exactly what parishes it covers from your National Library or from your local record office. One point you should remember is that the parishes covered in the district registers are civil parishes, not necessarily the same as the church parishes though they often coincide.

From the information which you have already collected you have to work out the years to search for information. You might know, for instance, the date of death of your grandfather but not know his age nor where he was born. You can obtain his age from his death certificate in the General Registry or from the District Registry and from this you can work out his approximate date of birth, remembering that the age is given by the informant at the time of death and is by no means always accurate.

If your grandfather or other ancestor died after 1865 you may not need to get a copy of the death certificate at all, because the age of the deceased is given in a column in the index. You are allowed to search all these indexes of death without paying any fee and, when you examine the indexes of death and find the required age and have then worked out the year of his birth, you can, after filling in a form for a search for a birth, examine these indexes. It is advisable to cover a few years either side of the calculated date of the age given at death since these are not always accurate. Start searching the index at the most likely year because this may prove more economical of your time. Covering as they do the whole of England and Wales, these indexes contain a great number of names and therefore each year is divided into quarters marked on the back with the last month of the quarter. To cover one year you have to search four volumes. You may be a bit surprised at the size of these indexes which are about two feet by eighteen inches. Even the modern ones weigh about eleven pounds and earlier ones, because they are parchment, weight approximately twenty-one pounds. So you will soon appreciate genealogy is at times physically as well as mentally exhausting!

You may be surprised that, even when your own surname is not too common, because of the great number of people in England and Wales you may find other people with exactly the same Christian name and surname as your ancestor. This may be a little confusing but you will have some rough idea where he was born, and the column which shows the district will indicate to a certain extent the possibility of this entry referring to your man or woman. But if you are searching for a really uncommon surname, then it may pay you to extract all the entries of that surname from the indexes, because from these you will be able to work out possible brothers or sisters and the likely date of marriage of their parents. These you can confirm by obtaining essential certificates, thus saving unnecessary expense in purchasing possible certificates. While the place where the birth took place will help, there are cases where identification becomes extremely difficult and has to be supplemented from other sources, such as wills. Certainly if you have got an unusual surname it has a great advantage. Even unusual Christian names, as already mentioned, can be a great help. People in earlier times seldom had more than one Christian name.

Anyway, assuming that you find in the index the entry which you feel convinced is the right one, you then fill in carefully the details from the index and take it to the official and pay the fee for the certificate. You can have it sent to you by post, in which case you write your name and address on an envelope given to you, or call for the certificate the next day. It is better, if convenient, to do the latter, because you get the information from it while still in London, and you will be able to use the information in it for possible further search in these or other records there.

Genealogists do find it annoying that they have to purchase an official certificate at full fee to obtain the information on it. Perhaps some day the authorities may be persuaded to allow genuine research workers to take copies of entries without further payment, at any rate for the entries of, say, a hundred years or more ago.

If you call for the certificate then, having got it, you will be able to work out your next step. If it is a birth certificate you may then want to obtain the marriage certificate of the parents. One difficulty is you will not know whether the birth certificate you have obtained is an elder child or a younger one, and therefore you may have to search back a considerable distance to get the parents' marriage. Nevertheless it will be a worthwhile search. You will get from the birth certificate the maiden name of the mother so that then, if it is a less common name, you can search for that name in the marriage indexes before you search for the husband's name.

But at some point you will be getting beyond the civil registration period and then you will have to turn to other records.

Chapter Four

CENSUS RETURNS

YOU MAY HAVE to consider at this stage what you should next examine; in other words whether you should go to census returns or to parish registers. If after searching the civil registration you have discovered that your family seems to have been established fairly firmly in one particular parish, then it might be best to search that parish register straight away. Even so, it might be advisable also to search the census returns later, in order to gather what additional information may be contained in them.

When it is not at all certain to which locality your ancestors belonged, then the census returns may prove invaluable and would have to be consulted. Once civil registration has been left behind, from the genealogist's point of view you have to remember that no census was made in England until the 19th century. In 1753 there was a proposal before Parliament to take a census but there was great opposition to it, some saying it exposed our weakness to possible enemies, while others opposed it on religious grounds, fearing it would cause the wrath of God to come down upon us, quoting from the Second Book of Samuel, the 24th chapter, in support of this. Parliament rejected this proposal.

The census, once started, was made every ten years. Those before 1841, however, if they had survived in detail, would have been no use to genealogists.

You will find as you progress that you must from time to time make intelligent guesses, and the ability to do this is one of the great assets in genealogy. Nevertheless, any conjectures of that nature must, of course, be confirmed later on with further evidence.

The 1851 census was far more valuable than the 1841, giving relationship to the head of the family, occupations and the parish in which persons were born. An annoying exception to the place of birth is of those who were born outside England and Wales, when the column will probably only say Scotland, Ireland or some foreign country.

One of the main problems in using the census return is finding the exact reference to the person concerned. This may, however, work out easier than it sounds. Probably one of the family was born on some date near that of the 1851 census and this will indicate where the parents were living then. The local directories may prove useful, though these often only give the householders. In the Guildhall Library in London there is a good collection of directories and usually the Library in the locality concerned has some local directories. In the larger towns there is sometimes an index of streets to the census returns so that you can discover easily in which volume of the returns your family will be found. In the case of smaller towns and villages there is probably no index, but at the beginning of each book there will be shown the parish and the street and area covered. If your ancestor was born in a village you may only be able to discover the name of the village in which he lived and no address. But it is not a very long job to search the census of a whole village, which may extend to three or four books. You get quite quick at picking out the name of a head of a family or a household. The amount you may learn about the village where your ancestor lived, the main occupations of the inhabitants and so forth will also be valuable when you come to write up the history of the family, which everybody should try to do. It always makes any family history more interesting if you can work in a little bit of the historical background rather than make your account of the family a string of bare facts. Learning something about your ancestors and the places where they lived is certainly a fascination attached to your family research. It helps to make it a living thing and not just a dry-as-dust affair which so many people, who know nothing about it, think it is.

Most of the census returns of today are seen on microfilm. They are housed in an annexe to the Public Record Office, in a house in Portugal Street.

Naturally there is an element of luck in hunting through these census returns. Sometimes they may give you quite unexpected information which will be of great value. You might find an elderly maiden aunt, or even a great-aunt, living with the family. If you did so, you might find this helped to take the pedigree farther back, because if you got, say, a maiden aunt aged 80, then the return would give her birthplace and you would know where she was born in approximately, say, 1771. It is important to remember that it is only approximate because when the census was made sometimes the information was given by one of the family who would not necessarily have a very exact idea of the great-aunt's age, or these aged relatives were quite capable of wishing not to reveal their exact age. But on the whole these returns seem to have been carefully made and are therefore particularly valuable. From them you will be able to go to the parish registers and places of birth indicated and perhaps find the family has been in that parish for generations. I know of somebody who was particularly fortunate in this way since he was able to trace his family back to the middle of the 16th century in a matter of a few weeks. But you must not always expect that kind of good fortune or you will be liable to disappointment.

The details which you discover in the census returns must, of course, be carefully recorded, and include any visitor and servant, for these can also prove valuable. Families often got their servants from their parents' or wives' parents' homes and the birthplace of the servant may indicate where the wife's family came from. Apprentices also living in the house of their master were sometimes relations and their birthplace may indicate another useful source.

Census returns can be seen up to 1881 at present, as they become available when they are over a hundred years old. These later ones are not so valuable as earlier ones because they are within the civil registration time, but in a case in which the whereabouts of a family cannot be found in the 1851 census but is known for the 1861, '71 or '81 census, then these returns will prove useful. The information in them is similar to that given in the '51 census return. It is rather unfortunate, though, that some of these later returns are in a far poorer physical condition than their predecessors.

There is no fee for inspecting census returns but you have to get a ticket to search them, which is a reasonable precaution to ensure that people who search them are responsible people who will respect the value of these records and treat them with care. Generally today you can only search them on microfilm. The information which you glean from these records will give you, if moderate fortune attends you, a considerable amount of further information about your family. Even with people of 50 years of age in 1851 the census will show you where they were born at the turn of the century and indicate a further place of search for you. In the ordinary way this will be the parish register and this valuable archive will be dealt with in the next chapter.

With the amount of work that is being done on genealogical sources a number of census returns have been transcribed and are held in local repositories for the particular area which the repository covers. You may therefore find that the census return of the area in which you are interested, or the parishes in which you are interested, will be held in the nearest local record office. In which case you will be able to search them possibly in greater comfort and nearer to your home.

Chapter 5

PARISH REGISTERS

YOUR NEXT STEP must now be the Parish Registers in which you can discover when your ancestors were born. If your ancestors were Church of England then, having discovered the parish or likely parish, your next step is to search it, which is fairly straightforward. Parish registers started as early as September 1538. The numbers that survive from that date are not large in comparison to the total number of Parish Registers.

In a small number of parishes the registers may still be held by the present incumbent. Others may be in the nearby County Record Office. Quite a number of registers have been transcribed or put on to microfilm and some of these transcripts will be held at the National Library of Wales or else at the applicable County Record Office in Wales. Also the Society of Genealogists in London has a number of parish register copies.

There is also the Mormon international genealogical index known as the IGI. This is an index made by the Latter Day Saints for religious purposes, but it can, of course, be valuable to genealogists. There is a list which tells you the parishes partly or wholly transcribed, and this is entitled *Parish and Vital Records: List of Genealogical Departments of Latter Day Saints*. The Mormons have not always been allowed to copy all the parish registers in a particular area and therefore the index is not complete, but they are nevertheless a useful finding aid. The entries are mainly concerned with baptism and marriages and rarely with burials. As far as Wales is concerned the whole of it is regarded as one entry and is therefore a complete index of the Principality, not merely indexes of individual counties in it, and this arrangement is very useful for you.

If you cannot find your own ancestors in the Welsh microfiche, then you must write or go to the County Record Office covering the area in which your parish is situated and discover from them whether there is any transcribed copy of it for the period you need, and if so, where it is located. If there is a transcribed copy it is easier to search and also you may find it is already indexed. Your local Family History Society may also help you in discovering your ancestors through a list of parishes in the county in which you are interested. Under a recent enactment most older parish registers have to be transferred to the nearest County Record Office. By their transfer they are not only made more accessible to searchers but they are also kept in really good condition, are able to be repaired where necessary, and generally are well looked-after in conditions of good security.

Make sure that the registers which you want to consult are there for the necessary period you require. If you are unable to visit the county record office, the record office may be able to undertake a search for you at a reasonable fee, but if you can manage to search the registers yourself this is desirable and more satisfactory, because you can then follow up any additional clues which may arise during your search.

Sometimes there is a hiatus in the parish register during the Civil War in the 17th century. Also during the Commonwealth which followed that war there was an enactment passed in 1653 that the births, marriages and deaths should be registered 'by some able and honest person' in a special book 'of good vellum or parchment'. This person was not the parish priest and it was in fact an attempt to set up a civil registration. In this respect you will notice it was the birth and death which were to be registered, not the baptism and burial. Very few, however, of these volumes survive. It is fortunate that in many cases the order was disregarded by the incumbent of the parish, who continued to record the baptisms, marriages and burials in his parish register as before. In some cases, however, you may find this gap just at a period when you least want it.

Do not forget when searching earlier parish registers that until 1 January 1752 the year began on 25 March, the Feast of the Annunciation, so that before that date any dates in January and February and in March up to the 24th came after December. People who have not realised this have been bewildered to discover a child born, for instance, in December 1740, being baptised in January or February 1740. Sometimes these dates are now written in the form '25 January 1734/5' signifying that the date was 25 January 1734 in the old style, and 25 January 1735 in the new style. Otherwise dates are normally put in the new style.

If the registers of the parish are missing or partly missing then there is always hope that the bishops' transcripts may survive. These were copies of registers which the incumbent was required to send in to the Diocesan Registry. In Wales the bishops' transcripts are all held in the National Library, where they can be consulted in comfort. It is unfortunate that a great many of these bishops' transcripts have been lost, or have survived but in very poor condition and may be very difficult to read. Forwarding them each year was just an additional irksome task for the incumbent, so that the less conscientious ones were not always to be relied on to forward them, particularly in the earlier periods. The surviving ones will be on sheets of paper. In copying, important details may have been omitted; this is fairly rare, and sometimes the opposite applies and details have been added which are not in the original registers. Ideally it is best to examine both the original and the transcripts.

You probably hope to trace your family back for many generations, perhaps even to the beginning of the registers themselves. But families before the 19th century did not always remain in the same locality as they have been thought to have done. Dr. Peter Spufford, Fellow of Jesus College, Cambridge, has studied the subject of population mobility very thoroughly and from his researches he has discovered that even quite ordinary people moved about in the past far more than is usually realised. Though poor people probably did not move very far, they seem to have moved about within the county perhaps as work took them to neighbouring places. The upper classes may have moved somewhat farther afield. If you find your line dies out in a parish, then you may have to look around in the neighbouring parishes, but people's movements depend on individual circumstances. It is a good idea to look at an old map and see where the road from your village led to and where was the nearest inn. Villagers would often walk up the road in search of refreshment and meet a father or brother of their future wife in the neighbourhood local. With a rare name it is a good idea to search for it in the wills of the period in the local court, usually the Archdeaconry court.

Chapter Six

NONCONFORMISTS IN WALES

THE WELSH, as you probably know, were great chapel people and nonconformists were strong in Wales. Nonconformity really began in England with John Wesley when he first of all formed a sect which still belonged to the Church of England but later broke away from it. One has to remember the many forms of nonconformity that existed in England. There were the Methodists who were a sub-division of the Wesleyan Methodists for a time, the Moravians, the Congregationalists and a number of minor denominations such as the Sandemans, the Campbellites, the Inghamites, the New Church, which comprised the Jerusalemites, or Swedenborgians, the Universalists, the Plymouth Brethren, the Quakers or Friends, and of course the Roman Catholics themselves. There were also some foreign churches in England of races who had migrated here from time to time. Among the earliest of these were the Walloons and Huguenots, then the Dutch churches, the Lutheran churches, the Swiss and Greek Orthodox churches.

The Calvinistic Methodists were a form of Methodism which was prevalent in Wales. The Calvinistic communities were divided into societies and sub-divided into bands and classes. They had both clerical and lay preachers and met monthly and quarterly. These Associations, as they were called, included not only the Whitfieldian societies in England but also the quite numerous societies in Wales. For quite a time the Calvinistic Methodists were linked with the Moravians, but in 1748 there was a division between Whitfield and the Moravians. Coinciding with this period Selina, Countess of Huntingdon, came into the field and became actively associated with the Calvinistic Methodists, and in 1751 Whitfield was appointed her chaplain.

However, the Whitfieldian societies did not accept the Countess of Huntingdon as their leader and in Wales they decided to elect Howell Harris: this rivalry between Whitfield and Harris divided the Welsh societies into two fields. About 1751, however, Harris withdrew from the Calvinistic Methodists.

Lady Huntingdon, through her own personal fortune and also through a number of gifts that were received by her, erected many chapels. Also, as she was a peeress, she had the right to appoint chaplains to herself and did so. These chapels were theoretically Anglican although the Anglican church was hostile towards them and the nonconformists themselves kept aloof.

Andrew Kinsman of Plymouth in 1763 built a Tabernacle in Devonport and declared it an independent church. He was later himself ordained in Broadmead Chapel, Bristol, by a number of Baptists and Congregationalists. In this way the Whitfieldian societies were the first Methodists to break with the Anclican church.

When Whitfield died in 1770 he left the leadership of the Calvinistic Methodists in England and Wales to the Countess of Huntingdon. However this caused a breach between the Whitfieldian societies and therefore a breach between them and the countess. The Tabernacle which was built in 1774 at Haverfordwest, in common with other chapels founded by the countess, was nominally Anglican. Later, because of difficulties that arose with the Anglican bishop, there was a break from the Church of England and the countess's connexion became a church of a Presbyterian type. The countess had also founded in 1767 a theological college near Trevecar, which had been Howell Harris' settlement in Breconshire. This college in due time became Cheshunt College, Cambridge. It is run by a separate body of trustees, and for that reason is not strictly a denominational college.

The Calvinistic Methodists grew considerably stronger in Wales than they did in England, mainly through the efforts of the local preachers, such as Howell Harris, Howell Davies and Daniel Rowlands. After Howell's withdrawal the leadership of the movement passed to Rowlands, but the Welsh Calvinist Methodists still remained part of the Anglican church until 1811, which is a much later date than that of other Methodist societies. It was mainly confined to Wales and the Welsh border counties of Herefordshire, Shropshire and Cheshire. When the Calvinist Methodist societies began to have their own churches, the term 'Methodist' to describe them fell into disuse. The Welsh Calvinistic Methodists were later called the Welsh Presbyterians or the Presbyterian Church of Wales. The record of survival of nonconformist records in Wales is not good. Many registers of dissenting congregations were deposited with the Registrar General after the Civil Registration Act was passed in 1836. These are now in the Public Record Office in London. But certain registers were not deposited and others were copied before they were sent to London. A number of these are now in the National Library of Wales. Other nonconformist records were not required to be handed in when civil registration was established. These include lists of members of churches. All these may often be of considerable genealogical value. Also various monthly publications of the nonconformist denominations quite often contain notices of births, marriages and deaths of nonconformists. They would often be connected with a particular church, but there might also be notes about members of other nonconformist religious bodies among them. Some of the more important of these journals were *Yr eurgrawn wesleyaidd* (Scren gomer 1818–; Baptist); *Y Diysorfa* (1831–; Calvinistic Methodist), *Yr Haul:* (1835–; Church in Wales); and *Y Diwy Giwr* (1835–; Congregational).

Although tracing the ancestry of nonconformists in Wales may have added difficulties through the absence of the nonconformist records, it may not be so bad as is first thought.

In the first place nonconformity, apart from such bodies as the Quakers, was not widespread until the 18th century and therefore before that time one should be able to trace the family in the surviving Anglican parish registers. Then again, nonconformists often continued to marry and have their children baptised in the Anglican church, and, when the Hardwicke Marriage Act of 1752 came into force, the only legal way in which you could be married (until civil registration came in 1837) was in the Church of England. Therefore you will find most congregationalists being married in their Anglican parish church. Similarly many of them had their children baptised, because again this was the only legal way to obtain a certificate for their birth. Such certificates were necessary, for instance, in various government appointments and also for proving your age in other spheres, such as for Naval passing certificates. When you went up for your examination for lieutenant you had to produce a baptismal certificate to show that you were 20 years of age and, although this was subject to considerable abuse, it was nevertheless valuable in many cases. Thus many nonconformists would have their children baptised in the Anglican church in Wales.

Then again, in the case of those who left wills or had administration granted for their estates which were proved in the courts (the ecclesiastical courts up to 1858 and after that in the civil probate courts), the beneficiaries needed proof of their birth and marriage in order to inherit.

Chapter Seven

WILLS AND ADMINISTRATIONS

SOME TIME FAIRLY EARLY in your research for family material you should be looking out for wills or administrations of your ancestors. A will is a personal testament, left by someone, and an administration exists where no will has been left and the person has died intestate. Wills can be most valuable, and also at times most frustrating, aids to information about your forbears. The first difficulty is in finding them, and then, when you have done so, you are often disappointed at the meagre information they reveal.

On the other hand, wills can reveal an enormous amount of information, and one of the intriguing merits is that they may open up all sorts of ancillary information which you never suspected and which you would never have come across unless you had searched these wills.

Do not imagine that it is only wealthy people who made wills. There are wills of people of all walks of life, some of whom left very little, perhaps only £5, though that amount in the past would have been worth very much more than it is today, about £100 in the 18th century.

Wills in England and Wales divided themselves into two distinct periods. The first period is that before 1858. Up to that date wills and administrations were proved or granted entirely by the Church. They would be proved in various ecclesiastical courts and the lowest of these was the archdeaconry court, in which the will or administration of a person whose estate was entirely in that archdeaconry could be proved or granted. Next came the consistory court, or the episcopal or diocesan court. A person who had property in two or more archdeaconries in the same diocese could have had his will proved, or his administration granted, in this court. Higher than the episcopal court came the two archbishops' courts. These were called 'Prerogative Courts', covering the province of the archdiocese. But Canterbury, being the senior archbishop's court, covered also the whole of England and Wales. Wales itself was in the province of Canterbury, and therefore people of substance in Wales would be likely to have their wills proved or administrations granted in the Prerogative Court of Canterbury (P.C.C.).

During the period of the Commonwealth the offices of bishops were abolished in 1646 and those of deans and canons, prebends, and so forth in 1649. Many wills during that period are found in the Prerogative Court of Canterbury.

Welshmen who died abroad, either in one of the Services or as a civilian, of any period, would be likely to have their wills proved in the Prerogative Court of Canterbury.

Those who had property in more than one diocese were bound to have their will proved in one of the prerogative courts, or if in two provinces, then in the senior prerogative court of Canterbury.

Although people with property in more than one diocese were obliged to have their wills proved in one of the prerogative courts, many people's wills were proved in the P.C.C. even when their property was in one diocese or even in one archdeaconry, because the P.C.C. had a high prestige and was regarded as a very efficient and safe court in which a will could be proved.

There is one other type of court which must be mentioned. This is the peculiar court. This court could consist even of only one parish, or possibly was confined to the boundaries of a manor, which had been granted these rights for some special reason, but often these peculiars were groups of parishes, or areas, which for some reason or other had been made into a peculiar. The will of anyone who died in the jurisdiction of a peculiar would have to be proved in that court, unless it was proved in a prerogative court. There were some peculiars attached to certain offices, such as the dean of a cathedral. A group of parishes might have been formed into a peculiar court for some reason in the past. The history of peculiars is an interesting study.

The Prerogative Court of Canterbury

The wills in this court are among the finest runs of inherited records. Wills and grants of administrations exist in this court from 1383 in an almost continuous run up to 1858, when Civil Registration started.

These P.C.C. wills and administrations, with inventories surviving in a number of cases, are held in the Public Record Office in Chancery Lane, London.

Inventories

This class of document has just been mentioned as possibly surviving among P.C.C. wills and administrations. It may also survive for the wills or administrations in any other courts. An inventory was a list of the goods of the deceased made by some official after the person had died. From these, if you are fortunate enough to find them among your own ancestors' wills, arises the possibility of gleaning a great deal about the testators' lives. For instance, from tools mentioned in the inventory, the trade of the testator can often be discovered. John West, in his delightful and informative book, *Village Records* [2nd edn., Phillimore 1982] has shown how you can even conjecture and possibly reconstruct the house in which your forbears lived, when these inventories mention the various rooms, and if the house should happen to have survived, you might be able to locate and identify and even visit the very house in which your ancestors once lived.

All these documents, being very personal, add flavour and body to the bare bones of a pedigree. You feel, in reading an ancestor's will and in examining his

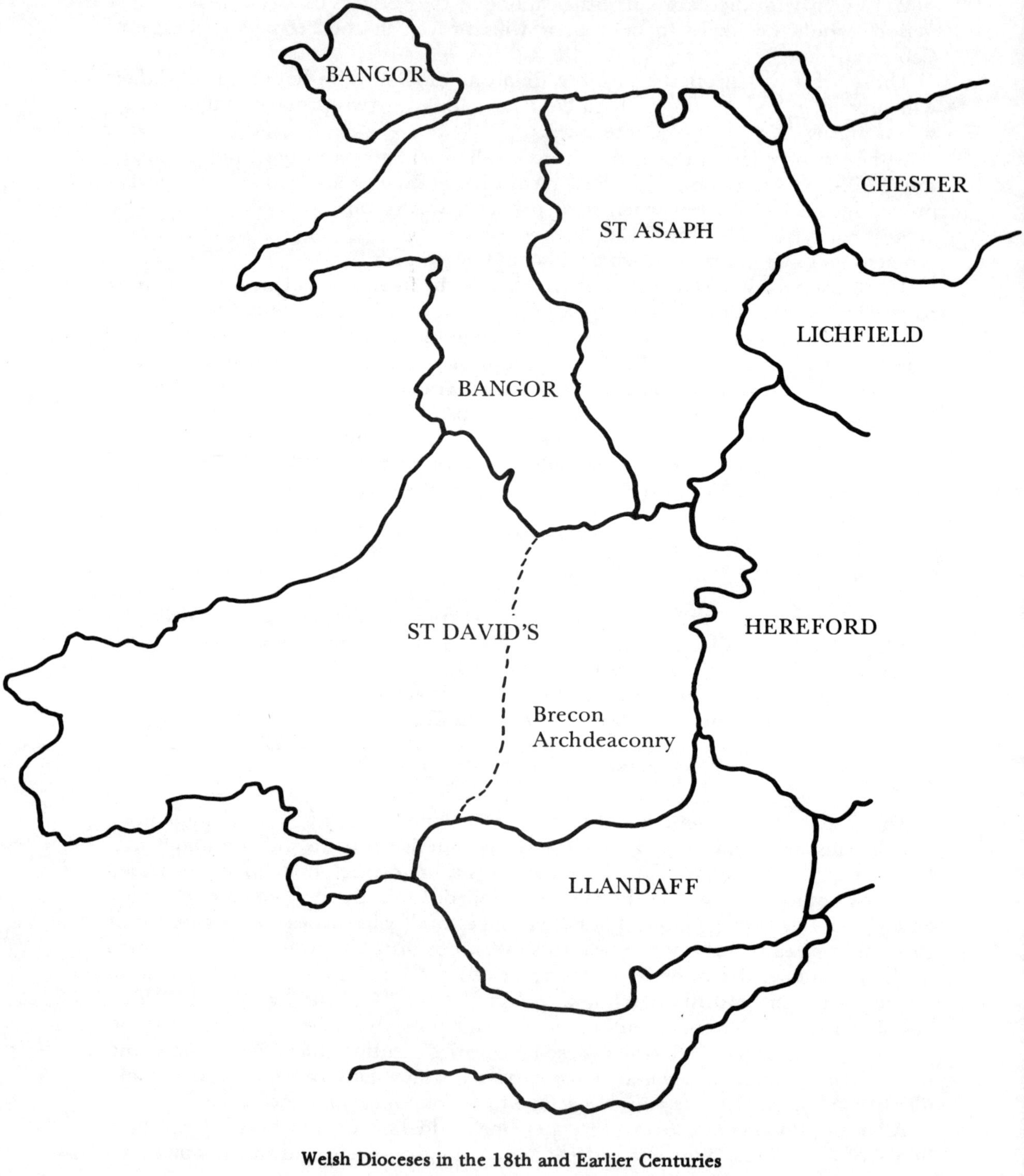

Welsh Dioceses in the 18th and Earlier Centuries

inventory, that you have been brought much closer to him than you were before. The will may be written in rather legal language, on the other hand it may be written without the help of a solicitor, in a very ordinary and colloquial style.

The Welsh Dioceses

In Wales itself there were certain variations to this general situation in England and Wales. There were only four dioceses, namely St Asaph, Bangor, St David's and Llandaff. Archdeaconry courts appear to have had little function in Wales, except for that of the archdeaconry of Brecon, which will be mentioned later. The archdeaconries of Cardigan and St David's appear to have retained only a slight degree of independence from the diocesan framework, which was centred at Carmarthen.

The archdeaconry of Brecon stood in a different position. Although regarded as an archdeaconry of St David's diocese, it was only contiguous with the eastern boundary of St David's and had an almost independent existence and a different standing from any other archdeaconry in Wales, almost as if it were a diocese itself.

Another Welsh variation from England was that the wills or administrations of ministers of the church and other men in holy orders were not required to be proved in the bishop's courts, as in England. They were treated in this connection as though they were laymen.

The full details of the holdings of the various dioceses in Wales are given in Anthony J. Camp's *Wills and Their Whereabouts* (1974), but the holdings of wills in the various courts in Wales have in some cases been moved since that book was published, some to the county record office of Hereford and Worcester, and others to that of Shropshire at Shrewsbury.

The details for the holdings of the four dioceses in Wales given below are therefore based on Anthony Camp's *Wills and Their Whereabouts* (1974 edn.) some additional information from Jeremy Gibson's *Simplified Guide to Probate Jurisdictions* (2nd edn. 1983), the useful *Guide to Genealogical Sources at the National Library of Wales*, and information up to the end of 1984 from the National Library, mainly of the movement of certain wills and administrations from that library to Shropshire and Hereford and Worcester record offices.

Before 1858

An outline of the holdings of the four dioceses in Wales is given below. Fuller details will be found, if needed, in Camp's book and in the other sources referred to earlier.

Episcopal Consistory Court of St Asaph

JURISDICTION:

The major parts of counties Denbigh, Flint and Montgomery, with the following parishes: Betws Gwerful Goch, Corwen, Gwyddelwern, Llandrillo, Llandderfel,

Llanfor, Llangar, Llangywer, Llansanffrald, Glyndyfrdwy, Llanuwchllyn, Llancil, Llanymawddwy, Mallwyd. (The deaneries of Mawddwy, Edeyrnion and Penllyn) in county Merioneth; Eglwys-rhos, Llangystennin and Llysfaen in county Caernarvon; Kinnerley, Knockin, Llanyblodwel, Llanymynech, Melverley, Oswestry, St Martin's, Selattyn and Whittington in county Salop.

Original wills, administrations and inventories exist from 1583, with many gaps until 1647. Then from 1660 to 1858, held in yearly bundles.

There are 13 volumes of register copy wills, each with an alphabetical index by Christian names. These volumes cover 1565 to 1709 with a number of gaps.

There are also 13 volumes of Act Books, starting 1584 but unindexed until 1670. From 1677 to 1820 they are indexed by Christian names and from 1821 to 1858 by surnames.

There are 11 volumes of indexes. The three earliest ones are indexed by Christian names, the remainder by surnames, the volumes covering 1729 to 1820.

There is also an alphabetical card index by surnames from 1729 to 1820. A microfilm of the indexes 1583 to 1729 is held by the Society of Genealogists in London. The wills are alphabetical by parishes after 1737.

Bangor Diocese

Episcopal Consistory Court

JURISDICTION:

Counties of Anglesey, Caernarvon (except parishes of Eglwys-rhos, Llangystennin, Llysfaen), Merioneth (except for 13 parishes in jurisdiction of Consistory Court of St Asaph), the parishes of Clocaenog, Derwen, Efenechdyd, Gyffylliog, Llanbedr Dyffryn Clwyd, Llandymog, Llanelidan, Llanfair Dyffryn Clwyd, Llanfwrog, Llangwyfan, Llangynhafal, Llanhychan, Llanrhaeadr-yng-Nghinmeirch, Llanrhudd, Llanynys and Rhuthun (the Deanery of Dyffryn Cllwyd) in county Denbigh, and the parishes of Carno, Llandinam, Llangurig, Llanidloes, Llanwnnog, Penstrowed and Trefeglwys (the Deanery of Arwystli) in county Montgomery.

There are very few surviving original wills from before 1635, but there are volumes of register copy wills and administrations before that date. Then three volumes: 1790 wills, 1851–57 wills and 1851–58 wills and administrations).

There are four volumes of indexes, 1655–99, 1700–89, 1790–1826 and 1827–58, the earliest in chronological order but the remainder alphabetical. There is also an alphabetical card index 1635–61.

St David's Diocese

Episcopal Consistory Court

JURISDICTION:

Counties of Pembroke, Cardigan, Carmarthen, and the parishes in county Glamorgan, in the Deanery of Gower, namely of Bishopston, Cheriton, Ilston,

Knelston, Llandeilo Tal-y-bont, Llanddewi, Llan-giwg, Llangennith, Llangyfelach, Llanmadog, Llanrhidian, Llansamlet, Loughor, Nicholaston, Oxwich, Oystermouth, Pennard, Penmaen, Penrice, Port Einom, Reynoldston, Rhosili and Swansea.

The original wills and inventories start in 1564 and continue with gaps to 1600; then are continuous 1600–53, and 1660–1858. There are also a number of unproved wills and administrations not completed and some bundles of inventories, mostly from the archdeaconry of Carmarthen. The archdeaconry of St David's, which includes South Pembrokeshire, has only a few surviving wills and administrations for the period 1629–48.

There are register copy wills from 1703 with gaps, and indexes for only part of the wills. There are also 13 Act Books, which include registers of administrations and wills received 1836–58, with other registers concerning Acts.

There are 10 volumes of general indexes, which cover, with some gaps, 1600–1858.

Recent work has been done to match up the inventories with the wills and administrations, but this difficult task has only been partially successful.

The archdeaconry of St David's consisted of the county of Pembroke, except for the northern quarter. The indexes to this diocese are largely only chronological lists.

Archdeaconry of Brecon

This archdeaconry is in the unusual position as being almost an independent court in dealing with its wills and administrations. It is known as the:

Consistory Court of the Archdeaconry of Brecon

JURISDICTION:

Counties of Brecon, Radnor (except parishes of Knighton, Michaelchurch-on-Arrow, Norton, Presteigne, New Radnor and Old Radnor), and the parishes of Cwm-iou, Llanthony and Oldcastle in county Monmouth, the parishes of Ceri or Kerry and Mochdre in county Montgomery, and the parishes of Clodock, Dulas, Ewyas Harold, Llancillo, Michaelchurch Eskley, Rowlston, St Margaret and Walterston in county Hereford.

The original wills begin in 1603, but are only regular from 1660 to 1858. Register copy wills in 26 volumes begin in 1570, but are irregular until 1694, then regular 1694–1858.

Llandaff Diocese

Episcopal Consistory Court of Llandaff

JURISDICTION:

Counties of Monmouth and Glamorgan (except for 23 parishes in the deanery of Gower in the jurisdiction of the Consistory Court of St David's. For names of parishes *see* that diocese).

The original wills in this diocese run from 1575 to 1858, with only the bundle for 1761 missing; nor is there a complete gap for the Commonwealth period, although there are very few wills registered in the period 1655 to 1659.

There are 35 volumes of register copy wills, covering the period 1695–1844.

The general indexes for this diocese are in three volumes, covering 1575–1799 alphabetical but incomplete, and 1799–1858 also alphabetical. These three volumes together therefore cover the period 1575 to 1858. The Society of Genealogists has a microfilm of these three volumes.

Peculiar Court of Hawarden

There has been only one peculiar court in Wales, the Peculiar of Hawarden, in Flintshire. The jurisdiction of this court was simply the parish of Hawarden. The original wills, administrations and inventories, 1554–1858 are in alphabetical bundles, and there are six Act Books, 1699–1858, with indexes in two of these Act Book volumes, namely 1752–1805 in Act Book no. 5 and 1805–57 in Act Book no. 6.

There is also a printed index to this peculiar in the *Publications of the Flintshire Historical Society*, volume 4.

The Joint County Record Office of Hereford and Worcester also holds in the Consistory Court of Hereford probate material covering a number of Welsh parishes. These are held in the County Secretary and Solicitor's Department, The Old Barracks, Harold Street, Hereford, HR1 2QX.

The Welsh parishes covered by this court are: Alberbury (part Salop), Buttington, Churchstoke, Forden, Hyssington, Mainstone (part Salop), Montgomery, Snead, Worthen (part Salop), Discoed, Knighton, Michaelchurch-on-Arrow, Norton, Presteigne, Old Radnor, New Radnor, Dixton and Monmouth.

1858 to Present Day

A will proved or administration granted from 12 January 1858 had to be proved or granted either in the Principal Probate Registry (now called the Principal Registry Family Division) at Somerset House, London, or at one of the District Probate Registries in England and Wales.

For wills and administrations made in the Principal Probate Registry the originals and the bound copies of the registered copies are held at Somerset House. For those proved or granted in the district registries the original will is kept in the district registry, but a copy of it is sent to Somerset House.

The General Index of Grants at Somerset House, and at many of the district registries, are printed annually, and this index gives all wills proved and all administrations made in the Principal Registry and in all district registries in England and Wales, and is thus a complete index made throughout England and Wales.

The National Library of Wales has the custody of register copy wills from the five registries for Wales, at St Asaph, Bangor, Carmarthen, Llandaff and Hereford. These cover Hereford and all but one of the Welsh counties, Montgomery.

Records of the last-mentioned county are held at Shrewsbury, and enquiries should be made to the Shropshire Record Office, County Hall, Abbey Foregate, Shrewsbury.

The National Library has MS indexes from 1858 for Llandaff (to 1905), Carmarthen (to 1923, with a card index 1924–1941) and Hereford (to 1928). St Asaph District has indexes in the volume of wills, 1860–1, and from 1858 to 1923. For Bangor only a card index, 1858–1935, is available.

If you are not able to visit Aberystwyth and search there for yourself, you can write to the librarian of the National Library, giving him as full details as you can of the ancestor whose will you seek, particularly the place where you think he died and the nearest date of his death. The staff at the National Library are very helpful.

You have to remember one important factor, and that is that surnames were adopted much later in Wales than in England, and patronymics continued up to the 17th century and in more remote parts, especially among people low down the social scale, they continued even until the 19th century. This means early indexes of wills are under Christian rather than surnames.

Another important factor which must be borne in mind is that the majority of people never left wills, nor do administrations exist for them. Those, of course, who left property in more than one diocese were bound to have their will proved in the Prerogative Court of Canterbury, and many people of substance would also have had their wills proved in that court. But with the poorer people there was no will left because they died with nothing, or practically nothing, to leave.

There is always the possibility, as happened in the more remote parts of Scotland, that in such areas in Wales a will was found, but it was never handed in for probate registration, but was just divided up amicably by the family in accordance with the bequests and terms in the will.

It must be remembered also that, by an Act of Parliament of 9 April 1653, a central court was established for the proving of wills and this covered the whole of England and Wales. These records, covering the years 1653 to 1660, were filed with the Prerogative Court of Canterbury wills in an unbroken series. These, as mentioned earlier, are preserved in the Public Record Office, the section in Chancery Lane, London.

The discovery of a will of an ancestor, as mentioned earlier, can be a source of great interest and information to you. It may also lead you to examine wills of other members of the family who may be mentioned in the particular will you have been examining. Often the wills of widows and maiden ladies give more information than the wills of a man with a family as the former will often mention nephews and nieces, or even more remote cousins and these may link up with other branches of the family and you can then trace their wills also.

This chapter gives you, I hope, an indication of the wills and administrations of the Welsh people, both those made or granted before 1858, when they were held by the Church and since then, when the Civil Registration of wills was introduced. It will be remembered that Welshmen of substantial estate were likely to have had their wills proved in the Prerogative Court of Canterbury during the church period. There is always also the possibility that the will of a

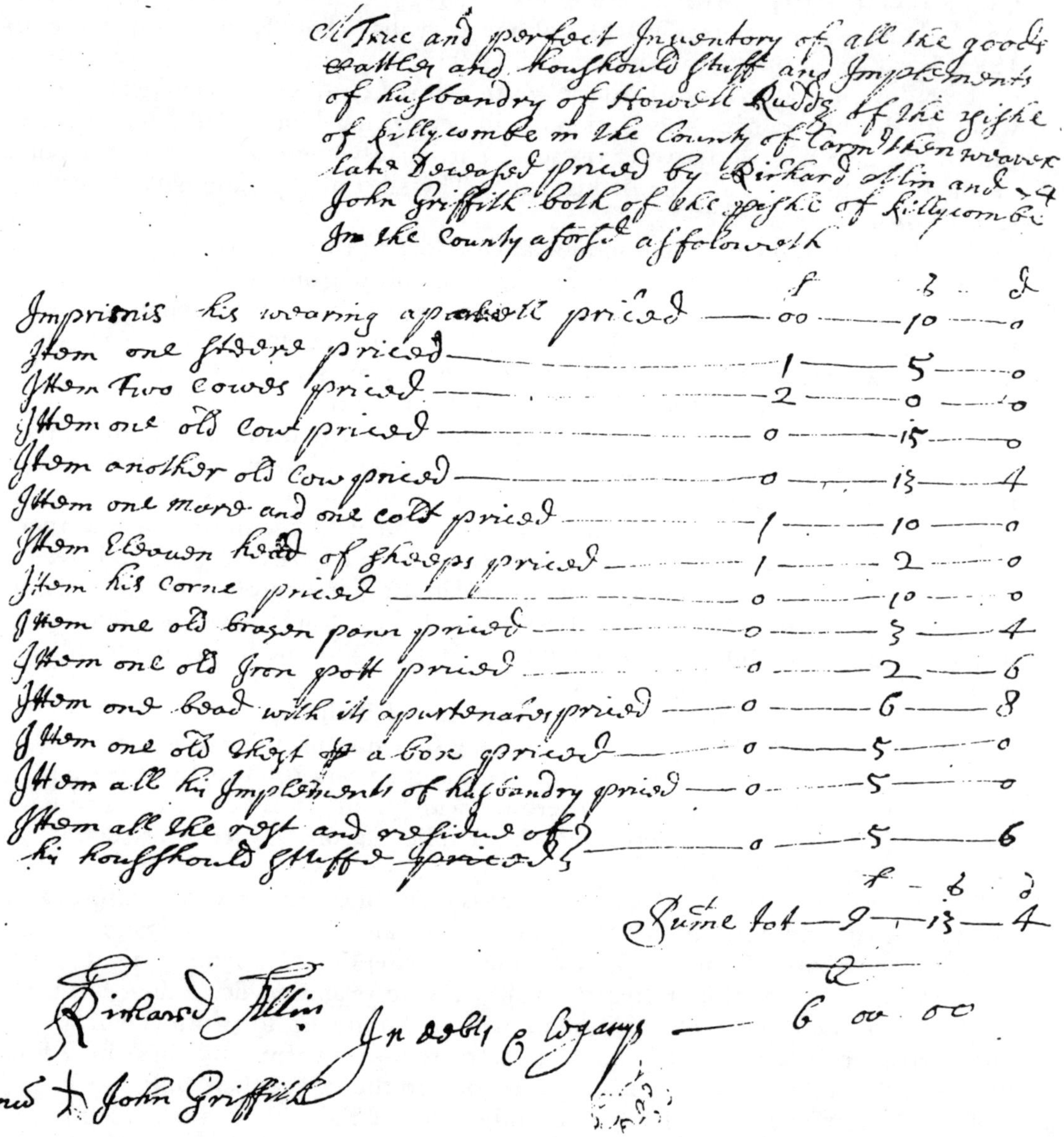

A True and perfect Inventory of all the goods Cattles and houshould stuff and Implements of husbandry of Howell Ruddg of the pishe of Killycombe in the County of Carmthen weaver late deceased prized by Richard Allin and John Griffith both of the pishe of Killycombe In the County aforsd as followeth

	£	s	d
Imprimis his wearing aparell priced	00	10	0
Item one steere priced	1	5	0
Item two cowes priced	2	0	0
Item one old Cow priced	0	15	0
Item another old Cow priced	0	13	4
Item one mare and one colt priced	1	10	0
Item Eleaven head of sheeps priced	1	2	0
Item his corne priced	0	10	0
Item one old brasen pann priced	0	3	4
Item one old Iron pott priced	0	2	6
Item one bed with its apurtenances priced	0	6	8
Item one old chest & a box priced	0	5	0
Item all his Implements of husbandry priced	0	5	0
Item all the rest and residue of his houshould stuffe priced	0	5	6
Sume tot	9	13	4
In debts & legacys	6	00	00

Richard Allin

signed + John Griffith

Inventory of Howell Rudderch, 1684/5.

A True and perfect Inventory of all the goods Cattles and househould stuff and Implements of husbandry of Howell Ruddz of the Pishe [parish] of Killycombe in the County Carm'then weaver late Deceased priced by Richard Alin and John Griffith both of the pishe [parish] of Killycombe In the County aforsd. as foloweth

	£	s.	d.
Imprimis his wearing aparell priced	00	10	0
Item one steere priced	1	5	0
Item two cowes priced	2	0	0
Item one old cow priced	0	15	0
Item another old cow priced	0	13	4
Item one mare and one colt priced	1	10	0
Item Elevean head of sheeps priced	1	2	0
Item his corne priced	0	10	0
Item one old brazen pan priced	0	3	4
Item one old iron pott priced	0	2	6
Item one bead with its apurtenanes priced	0	6	8
Item one old shert & a box priced	0	5	0
Item all his Implements of Husbandry priced	0	5	0
Item all the rest and residue of his housshold stuffe priced	0	5	6
Sume tot.	9	13	4

Richard Allin
Signed John Griffith In Debts & legacys 6 00 00

In the name of god Amen, the seaventh Day of March in the yeare
of our lord god one thousand six hundred eighty five according to the
Computation of the Church of England I Howell Ruddz of the pishe of
Killycombe in the County of Carthen weaver, being sick of body but of
perfect memory praised be to god, doe make and ordaine this my
last will and testament in manner and forme followinge first
I bequeath my soul Into the hands of Almighty god my maker, hoping
that through the meritorious Death and passion of Jesus Christ my only
saviour and redeemer to receive free pardon and forgivenesse of
my sins; and as for my body to be buried in Christian buriall at
discretion of my executor hereafter nominat Imprimis I give unto
my nephy Ruddz william two steers of three yeares old Item I give
unto my nephy Ruddz Rees two heifers, one of three years old another
of one yeare, Item I give unto ~~David William~~ Elianor Rees my neece five
shillings with her grandmothers chest Item I give unto my neece
Katherine Owen one heifer of two yeare old, with [illegible] shillings
Item I give unto my nephy John Rees three shilling four pence
Item I give unto my godson John Morgan three shillings Item
I doe nominat and appoint Gwenllian Rees my now wife to be my
executor of all the rest of my goods cattles and household stuff
upon condition that shee shall pay all my Depts and legacis; and I
make her sole executor of this my last will and testament, revoking
all other wills and testament In wittnesse hereof I have hereunto sett my hand
and fixed my seale ~~dated~~ the day and yeare first above written

Sealed and Delivered in
the sight and presence of

Howell Ruddz
HR

Signd James William
Signd Rees william
Signd Morgan Thomas
Morgan David

26° Martij 1684
Insinuatur hoc testum una cum tabulas
testamentarias coram [illegible]
me

Tho Bevan.

Will of Howell Rudderch, 7 March 1684/5.

In the name of God Amen, the seaventh Day of March in the yeare of our lord god one thousand six hundred eighty five according to the Computation of the Church of England I Howell Ruddz [Rudderch] of the pish [parish] of Killycombe in the County of Car[mar]then weaver being sick of body but of perfect memory praised be to god, doe make and ordaine this my last will and testament in maner and forme folowing first I bequeath my soul Into the hands of Almighty god my maker, hoping that through the meritorious Death and passion of Jesus Christ my one Saviour and redeemer to receive free pardon and forgiveness [of] my sins and as for my body to be buried in Christan buriall att the Discression of my Executor herafter nominat Imprimis I give unto my nepuhy Ruddz William Two stears of threee yeares old Item I give unto my nephy Ruddz Rees Two hifers, one of three years the other of one yeare Item I give unto Eleanor Rees my neecie five shillings with her grandmothers Chest Item I give unto my nee[ce] Phathering Owen one hifer of two yeare old, with tenn shilling[s] Item I give unto my nephy John Rees three shillings four peence Item I give unto my godson John Morgan three shillings Item I Doe nominat and appoint Gwenllian Rees my now wife to be my Exe[c]utor of all the rest of my goods Cattles and houshould stuffe Upon Condition that shee shall pay all my Depts and legacis and I make her Executor of this my last will and Testament, revoking all other wills and Testament In witness hereof I have hereunto sett my [hand] and fixed my seale the Day and yerie first above written.

Sealed and Delivered in)
the sight and psence of) HOWELL RUDDZ

sigd James Abraham
sigd Roger William
sigd Morgan Thomas
Morgan David

26 Martii 1684
Infinewtur hoc testum &c.
Coram me

Tho Bevan

Welshman may have been proved in some other court, perhaps in some other peculiar outside Wales, because the testator held some property in that area.

People seeking Welsh ancestors are fortunate in having nearly all their wills and documents of administration, and of any inventories existing, held in the National Library of Wales. This very often makes the search for wills of Welshmen rather simpler than for wills in England. You should keep careful record of the wills you have found. It is unnecessary to take down every detail of a will, which may be long-winded and have many repetitions, and I have suggested in my book *In Search of Ancestry* (4th edn., p. 40), that you should keep extracts of wills on 8 x 5 slips, which conveniently can be stored in drawers of that size.

Anthony Camp's *Wills and Their Whereabouts* has an excellent introduction, interestingly written, which tells you almost everything you need to know about wills throughout their history, the way in which a will was made and variations that occur during the centuries, what happens if a person to whom a bequest is made has died before the testator, the disposal of land in wills, what is meant by personal property, what happens if a will is not witnessed or properly witnessed, or if there was no executor appointed. His book also tells you to what extent the wills of each court have been indexed, and in fact is a valuable guide to the complications of finding a will in the days before 1858 when they were proved in the church courts.

When searching for wills, you must remember that variation in spelling before about 1800 was considerable. Many people were not well educated and others also spelt phonetically rather than with any exact spelling of names and words.

There are many printed indexes of wills produced by various associations or societies, particularly by the Index Society and the British Record Society. There are also many MS indexes of wills in a number of libraries and record offices. It may be interesting to mention here that the Society of Genealogists in London has a slip index of the wills of the Prerogative Court of Canterbury from 1750 to 1800, which they will search for a small fee. Already three volumes of this index have been published, covering wills of persons with names from 'A' to 'G' and further volumes of this index will be published in due course.

Wills can reveal an enormous amount of information.

Chapter Eight

PROFESSIONAL MEN

CLERGYMEN of the church in Wales would in many cases be graduates of either Oxford or Cambridge universities and their parentage is found easily through the matriculation registers of these two universities, which give the father's name and place of residence and sometimes details of the son's career.

The volumes of *Alumni Oxonienses*, edited by Joseph Foster, cover the matriculations from 1500 to 1886 and the Cambridge registers, *Alumni Cantabrigienses*, cover the period from the earliest times to 1900. Both give the name and occupation of the father and the place where the father belonged which is often the birthplace of the son; and also some biographical details about the undergraduates themselves and their further career, their degrees, and particularly if they themselves were ordained. They sometimes give the name of a wife. They also often link up the person with any other relations at the university. If, however, the clergyman did not go to Oxford or Cambridge, as was sometimes the case with those who were ordained later in life, then the ordination papers will or should give you a certified copy of the ordinand's baptismal entry. These papers are probably held either by the applicable Welsh County Record office or by the National Library of Wales.

There are lists of clergy from the early 19th century which give varying details of the persons concerned, officially known as Clerks in Holy Orders. *Crockford's Clerical Directory*, although only started in 1858, is quite often useful for later members of the church. There is also Joseph Foster's *Index Ecclesiasticus*, which gives clerical appointments for the period 1800 to 1840. It should also be mentioned that clergymen are particularly mentioned in the *Gentleman's Magazine*, which ran from 1731 to 1864.

Nonconformist Ministers

Information about ministers of other denominations is more difficult to trace, but there are lists of such clergy for many of the denominations, although they do not go back very far. The Methodists have indexed the biographical obituary notices of their ministers from 1778 to 1839 appearing in their *Armenian* and *Methodist* magazines. The Congregational Union of England and Wales have obituaries of their ministers in their Year Book and these are often quite full. They do not go back far.

The Congregationalists are one of the earliest bodies of nonconformism. They suffered under many disabilities for a long period. The Conventicle Act of 1664 forbade religious meetings, except those of the Anglican church. The Five Mile Act forbade nonconformist ministers from teaching in schools, and in 1673 the Test Act ordered that every person holding office under the Crown should take the sacrament according to Anglican rites.

A gradual adoption of more relaxed conditions came about during the 18th century and ministers like George Whitfield roused the conscience of many of the established church leaders. The National Union of Congregational Churches, founded in 1832, did a considerable amount towards preserving their records.

Methodist Ministers

The official archives of the Methodist movement are in the Methodist Bookroom, City Road, London. Information about methodist ministers, as well as individual methodists who were prominent in the movement, can be obtained from the movement's magazine, which began as the *Armenian Magazine* in 1778 and then changed its title to *The Methodist* from 1798 until 1821, and then the *Wesleyan Methodist Magazine* ran from 1822 to 1913. You nearly always found an obituary of a particular minister in these magazines and there is an index to memoires and to local histories published in the *Proceedings of the Wesleyan Historical Society* from 1778 to 1839 in volume VII (pp. 99–100). Various branches of the Methodist movement have also published their magazines.

Quakers

The Society of Friends, known as Quakers, were from early times conscious of the importance of keeping records. These were handed over to the authorities in accordance with the 1840 Act, but before they did so they made details of the information in the form of digests, and these are at The Friends House in Euston Road, London, NW1. One has to get used to the unusual dating of the Quakers, such as that January is 'first month' and Sunday is 'first day' and so forth. These registers are described by J. S. Rowntree in his *Friends Registers of Births, Deaths and Marriages, 1650–1900.* All these digests continue to 1837 in England and Wales.

Roman Catholics

The Roman Catholic registers were not deposited under the 1840 Act. They obtained permission not to do so. You therefore have to apply to the Roman Catholic Church to find out what records survive of their ministers.

This is also true of the Jews who were also exempted from the requirements of the Act, and their registers have also been kept by their own communities.

A number of Welsh Nonconformist chapel registers were also not deposited, and most of these are now in the National Library of Wales.

Lawyers

Many Welsh people in the legal profession would have had to qualify in England. There are two main groups in the legal world, barristers and solicitors. A solicitor is not able to be a member of the Bar and similarly a barrister cannot be enrolled as a solicitor.

Tracing the parentage of barristers is comparatively easy. A barrister had to be admitted to one of the Inns of Court which today are Lincoln's Inn (particularly specialising in Chancery practice), the Middle Temple, the Inner Temple and Gray's inn. On entering these Inns a man had to give certain particulars about himself, which included his parentage, and usually also a description of his father's occupational status and place of residence. All Inns except the Inner Temple have published fairly complete admission registers, so that information is usually obtainable from them. In the case of the Inner Temple the admissions for the period 1547–1660 have been published, but for later admissions one must write to the Librarian for information. This Inn lost some records during the Second World War, but the admission registers survived.

Parentage of solicitors, who used to be known as attorneys, can be traced through the Articles of Clerkship, which exist from 1780–1838 in the Public Records Office in Chancery Lane, London. These are arranged by date of entry into Articles, but there is a manuscript alphabetical index to the names. Additional Admissions books cover 1729 to 1848, and then another series from 1838 to 1860, which are also in the Public Record Office. Solicitors in earlier times might be articled locally for a period to allow them to qualify. The indexes at the Society of Genealogists for apprentices contain people who were apprenticed to attorneys just as other apprentices. These indexes give details of father's name and profession or occupation, and the name of the attorney to whom the boy was apprenticed and the fee paid. Dates can also be traced through law lists, from which you can usually discover when a solicitor died. You should then be able to find his will proved in one of the Welsh courts or from the Prerogative Court of Canterbury in London.

As judges were all taken from the ranks of barristers their parentage can be traced in the same way as for barristers. You can also find them in Foster's *Judges of England* and possibly in such works as the *Dictionary of National Biography*.

Magistrates (or J.P.s) are laymen appointed by the Lord Chancellor. Records of appointment are among the Lord Chancellor's records, and many county record offices in Wales will have lists of J.P.s for various periods; also during later periods, as in the 19th century, they can be traced from local directories. Information about various officials in the Law Courts can be traced in such works as the *Royal Calendar* which exists from the late 18th century onwards.

Medical Men

Medical men who are graduates can be traced through the University records, which will sometimes give their parentage. But it is more difficult to trace others.

In earlier times the medical world was divided into two main division, physicians and surgeons. Physicians were regarded as higher in status and were often university men with degrees in medicine, or members of the College of Physicians, and can be traced by the University or College records.

The surgeons until 1745 were in London linked with the barbers in the Surgeons' and Barbers' Company which was one of the livery companies of London. After that date their status was improved and by 1800 the Royal College of Surgeons was founded. But even at the beginning of the 19th century surgeons were socially below the position of physicians. Their work was not the carrying out of operations by men specialised in surgery, but they performed simple functions as general practitioners of medicine and dentistry, setting bones, pulling out teeth and serving as general medical advisers and apothecaries. They were socially somewhere between tradesmen and professional men. Even physicians were not regarded as very much higher than attorneys. In earlier times a young man might be apprenticed to a local surgeon for five years in the way that John Keats, the poet, was. You may find his parentage in the previously mentioned index to the apprentices at the Society of Genealogists for the period from 1710 to 1760.

Surgeons were very often licentiates of the Society of Apothecaries, and as that body was one of the City Livery Companies, a certain amount of information can be discovered from the Company records, now in the Guildhall Library, London. They give the name and occupation of the father and other details, such as the names of referees, and as these references were sometimes from the local vicar or rector, this often indicated the place from which he came; another certificate had to be obtained to show that he was more than twenty years of age. Monk's roll of physicians should not be overlooked though this only covers rather well-known medical men. Medical directories began in the early 19th century and these tell you where a practitioner was in practice and, in the volume of the year in which he died, there may be a short obituary of him. Some later directories may give a brief account of those listed, giving their qualifications. However doctors are less likely to have qualified in Wales at this period. Many of them did so in Scotland, or Ireland or abroad, such as Leiden in Holland, of which a list of English students has been published. Information may also be obtained from the Scottish University records, Glasgow being particularly good for this purpose. Medical men in the army and navy and East India Company can be traced in the records of those services, in which they were known generally as surgeons, the term physician being used for more important posts.

Other Professions

Records of these vary considerably and it is only possible to give a very brief account of them. Tradition is certainly strong in many occupations, the theatrical profession, for example, produced many families like the Forbes Robinsons, the Terrys and Keans, John Gielgud and the Redgraves, who had numerous relatives in the profession. *Who's Who in the Theatre* is a useful modern guide, and from this you can see how many actors tended to be sons of actors and to have married actresses. In the *Genealogists' Magazine* of December 1933 there is an article by Dr. J. M. Bullock on 'Theatrical Families'.

Sir George Grove's *Dictionary of Music and Musicians*, which was originally published in four volumes and has now been expanded to 20 volumes, gives considerable information about distinguished musicians.

For architects, H. M. Colvin's *Biographical Dictionary of English Architects 1660–1849* is useful. Details of men who served in the Customs and Excise offices during the 18th century may be found from the Establishment records in the Public Records Office. Work is being done on the History of Parliament; Romney Sedgewick's two-volume *The House of Commons 1715–1754*, published in 1970, has much biographical information about members and this is continued by Sir Lewis Namier and John Brooke's *House of Commons 1754–1790*, in three volumes, the third of which is biographical information about the members themselves. Then Joshua Wilson's *The Present House of Commons* deals with the House at the time of Trafalgar in 1805.

Samuel Redgrave's *Dictionary of Artists of the English School*, first published in 1874, gives an account of artists of the 19th century and M. H. Grant's *Dictionary of British Etchers* and his *Dictionary of British Sculptors* is also useful. Authors are covered by various publications and their careers can be traced to a certain extent by noting their publications in the British Catalogue.

A Fusilier of the mid-18th century of the 23rd Foot, or Welch Fusiliers.

Chapter Nine

ARMY AND NAVY RECORDS

THE RECORDS OF these services are held in the Public Records Office. Naturally it is easier to trace officers than men in the ranks, but the material about them all is considerable, though they do not to any extent go back, in a biographical sense, earlier than the beginning of the 18th century. The manuscript of Lieut.-General Henry George Hart, who was the compiler of *Hart's Army List*, and who had been working on an army biographical dictionary, is held in the Public Records Office at Kew and is in WO211/2-6. The manuscript contains detailed biographical accounts of the general and field officers compiled by him for his projected *Army Biographical Dictionary*.

There are a great many regimental histories, which vary greatly in quality; the best of them are very good, sometimes giving complete accounts of all officers who served in the regiment. An early series of regimental histories is that by F. Cannon, but many later histories are more accurate and more comprehensive. The *Institute of Army Historical Research Journal* contains many articles and information about regiments, their officers and men. It is important to discover what regiment or corps the person for whom you seek information was in. An officer can be traced fairly easily through the army lists. These exist in manuscript in the PRO from 1702 onwards (WL64) and the lists have been printed annually since 1754 with an isolated issue of 1740. Also Charles Dalton's *English Army Lists and Commission Registers 1661-1714* in six volumes and his *George I's Army* are both informative about an earlier period. The 13 volumes of Sir John W. Fortescue's *History of the British Army* are well indexed and contain references to hundreds of officers and men. An officer's career can be traced from volume to volume through the army lists, noticing his promotions and the rank which he reached. You may find a note of his death in the pages of Casualties. There is always a possibility, however, that he sold his commission and, if so, you should find a reference to this also.

But you do not get information about an officer's personal life, his marriage and children until the 19th century. The 1828 return of officers retired on full pay and half pay, and the 1829 return of those on active full pay, are specially valuable for this detailed information. The half-pay return gives, among other items, the age on first appointment, the date of that and the regiment in which commissioned and successive promotions and dates, whether he was placed on half pay by reduction or purchase of a half-pay commission etc., and often if he is desirous of further service, and the total length of service on full and half pay. Then you get details of whether he was married and, if so, the date and place of the marriage and the general place of residence during the last five years.

The 1829 full-pay return (WO25 and WO76) gives all the above details with some important additions: the place and date of birth, whether the first commission was obtained by purchase or otherwise, details of any campaigns in which the officer had taken part; an account of service abroad; if married, details of place, date and name of wife, and indication if she is still alive; names of legitimate children, with their date of birth and place of baptism, total of service, divided into time abroad and time at home.

There is a later return of service of officers on full pay and on half pay of 1847. This is less valuable, being more recent and referring only to retired or half-pay officers. It can prove quite useful in filling gaps concerning an officer's service. In the 18th century the War Office sent out instructions that officers were to give details of their marriage when they took place. These are useful in giving the officer's name on marriage, the name and age of the bride, the place and date of the ceremony and the names of the officiating clergyman and the witnesses. These returns are in WO25 at the Record Office at Kew. There are also at the PRO card indexes for half-pay returns of 1828 and for officers' marriages from about 1810, and another, in progress, of officers' services of 1829 onwards.

A very valuable record of officers is the *Commander-in-Chief's Memoranda*. This gives details of an officer's application for commission, by whom it was recommended, and of the approval of the Colonel of the Regiment. It also shows whether the officer was recommended for a commission with purchase or without purchase. Often those who were sons of serving officers, or of officers who had been killed, and therefore of officers' widows, were given commissions without purchase. In the *Commander-in-Chief's Memoranda* you may find letters of the officer recommending him and often mentioning any other relatives which he has had in the army.

The Royal Military Academy at Woolwich, which opened in 1741, has records of its cadets for the period 1799 to 1805 and from 1820 to 1839. It continues with some gaps until its closure. The Royal Military College at Sandhurst, now named the Royal Military Academy, was opened in 1812. Records of admissions of cadets from that date are held here as are the Woolwich records also.

The Sandhurst records give the date of the cadet's admission, age on admission, his height, father's name and rank or occupation, and the date of his leaving the college, with various remarks as appropriate. The Woolwich Royal Military Academy records gives similar details. Both can be obtained from the Librarian, Central Library, Royal Military Academy, Sandhurst, Surrey, GU15 4PQ. The surviving Records of all regular other ranks prior to 1901, which were previously held at Army Records Offices, have now been transferred to the PRO. Unfortunately records of non-pensioners before 1883 were accidentally destroyed by fire a number of years ago. In these cases you can get an idea of a man's service from the various Muster Rolls, which also give you the parentage of the man at the date when he enlisted. It is therefore important to know in what regiments an ancestor served. In searching the Muster Rolls you should find there when he enlisted, his place of birth and possibly his trade, if he had one, or occupation. Once you have discovered this you can then go on through the Muster Rolls, tracing his career and where he served.

When an officer or man died there was usually some portion of pay due to him, even if, as an officer, he was on half pay, and its disposal can be discovered from the pay book which may be helpful. If he left a will this will probably be proved in the Prerogative Court of Canterbury, or, if not, then there will be an administration in the Prerogative Court of Canterbury dealing with the pay due to him at the time of death. This will usually indicate to whom it was paid; perhaps his wife, if he was married, and so you will discover his wife's name and where she was living at the time.

Many Welshmen have served in the British Army and a number of regiments are particularly attached to Wales. The Welsh Guards was the most recently established of the Guards regiments, and they have quickly become a competitor with the other guards regiments for smartness and efficiency, and a number of Welshmen have joined them. In the Cavalry the 3rd Dragoon Guards are the Prince of Wales' Dragoon Guards, the 10th Dragoon Guards are known as the Prince of Wales' Hussars, and the 12th Regiment of Cavalry are the Prince of Wales' Royal Lancers. Of infantry regiments the 23rd is the Royal Welch Fusiliers and the 41st is the Welch Regiment, and another well-known Welsh Regiment is the 82nd or Prince of Wales' Volunteers. Though they are described as a volunteer regiment, as originally they may have been, they have long been a regular infantry regiment.

Navy Ancestors

With a seafaring nation like Great Britain you may well find some of your Welsh forbears in the Royal Navy. The main manuscript sources for the navy are the Admiralty Records in the Public Record Office at Kew. Taking first of all the records of officers, there are a number of useful biographical volumes. There is John Charnock's *Biographia Navalis* or *Memoires of the Officers of the Navy from 1600*, which was published in 1794 in four volumes, and John Campbell's *Lives of British Admirals*, also four volumes, published in 1779 and, as its title implies, confined to Flag Officers. The *Naval Biography of Great Britain* by James Ralfe (1828) is a fairly rare work which includes some officers which are not found in other works. We then get on to John Marshall's *Royal Naval Biography* which is more useful because it covers a wider scope. It runs into 12 volumes and claims to cover all officers who reached the rank of Commander, who were living or had only recently died in the period from 1823 to 1830. All of these works give details of an officer's career – with particular mention, of course, of any actions in which he may have taken part – and also, usually, of his parentage.

But the most comprehensive work published on naval officers is W. R. O'Byrne's *Naval Biographical Dictionary*, published in 1849. This includes every officer of the rank of lieutenant and above who was serving, or retired and living, in the year 1845. This notices some 5,000 officers, and in many cases the father is also mentioned and frequently any other relative who may have served in the navy.

It is also useful that the manuscripts of the Returns for this book which the various officers made, together with their letters, are in the British Museum (Additional MS 38039/54). These, therefore, often give more information than is contained in the printed work. There was a second edition of O'Byrne's work issued in parts, but this is unfortunately incomplete, only going as far as the name H. G. S. Giles, and its date of publication (1861) makes it less valuable. On the other hand it is more comprehensive than the earlier edition, as it included all Royal Marine officers, surgeons, chaplains and pursers.

An officer's career can, of course, be traced through the various Navy lists. Steel's List was first published in 1772 and the Official List began in 1814. Another useful publication is the National Maritime Museum's *Commissioned Sea Officers of the Royal Navy*. This is in three volumes, and includes brief dates of promotions of officers from the earliest times until 1815.

Regarding officer manuscript records, the Admiralty Records at the PRO at Kew, described in volume 2 of the 1963 edition of the *Guide to the Public Record Office*, are also listed in the PRO lists and indexes XV III (HMSO, 1904), to which there is a supplementary typescript on the shelves of the PRO at Kew.

A useful small book is Gerald Fothergill's *Records of Naval Men* published in 1910. It was brought out particularly to be read in conjunction with the official Lists and explains the type of information found in those records.

One of the best sources for officers' parentage is in the Lieutenant's Passing Certificates series from 1789 onwards (with a few earlier examples from 1777). The Navy Board copies have filed with them the baptismal certificates which had to be produced to show that candidates were at least twenty years of age. There are two manuscript indexes to them at the Record Office at Kew. One of these is by Miss B. H. B. Fairweather, covering the years 1777 to 1832, and includes the information from the baptismal certificates, and therefore this obviates the need to look at the original documents unless you particularly want to do so.

Another useful source is Sir William Clowes' *Royal Naval History*. The eight volumes of this work are individually well indexed and refer to hundreds of naval officers and ratings in their account of the history of the navy.

Memorials submitted by men who were wounded can give an account of a person's career, and details of courts martial will also reveal much. For officers there are also various returns of service, although they do not start before the 19th century. The Return of 1817 includes all the officers serving then. This is a valuable return, from which you can obtain the officer's naval career up to that date.

Ratings

The most important records for tracing the parentage of a rating are the ships' muster rolls. For a rating entering a ship, particularly his first ship, his birthplace will be given. It should also be remembered that midshipmen and volunteers, later cadets, were not commissioned officers, but were regarded as subordinate officers. They therefore counted as ratings and for that reason their birthplace was also given when they joined a ship. So, if you trace an officer's career back to the time when he was a midshipman, you can find his place of birth, if by any chance his baptismal certificate, at the time he took his Lieutenant's passing examination, should be missing. It must be mentioned, however, that some of these places of birth are inaccurate: also, the baptismal certificates produced to show that a midshipman was 20 years of age when he went up to take his examination 'for Lieutenant' were sometimes faked, to show that he was 20 when in fact he was less than that. Also, if for any reason age is stated on other returns, it may be inaccurate, since once a person had given his age as higher than it was, it had to continue in his records as such. Both Nelson and Collingwood provide examples of false ages in their records. Bounty papers covering the period 1675–1822 give the name and address of the relations to whom the bounty is to be paid in the case of seamen who had been killed in action or had died while serving. Sometimes certificates of baptism of the next of kin and parents' marriage certificates exist among records to prove relationship with a seaman. These include both officers and other ratings.

It will be noted that most of these records belong to the period starting towards the end of the 18th century. The survival of records earlier than that time is less good. These earlier records are also seldom well indexed. The diarist Samuel Pepys was himself Secretary of the Navy and his collection, now at Magdalene College Cambridge, covers the proceedings of the Admiralty and the Navy Board from 1673 to 1679, and Pepys' *List of Commissioned Officers* is particularly valuable in giving the name, rank and ship of almost every officer serving between 1660 and 1688. These have been included in the *Commissioned Sea Officers* referred to earlier. Other records which may prove valuable are the Captains' Letters in the Secretary's Departments, and the Lieutenants' Letters, which often contain letters of application for appointments to ships, and perhaps give the home address of the officer. Then the series of letters termed 'Promiscuous' may be about almost any subject, sometimes from creditors trying to get in touch with an officer who owes them money. The letters and records from the Royal Naval College Portsmouth, which began in 1773, are useful as they often give reports of scholars' progress, usually mentioning one parent's name and the dates and reason for the cadet's discharge. The Greenwich Hospital records are also useful, covering as they do both 'In' and 'Out' pensioners, the school, apprenticeship of children of seamen, and matters such as the children at Clarence House, Paddington Green. These are invaluable for information about any persons admitted to this foundation, whether officers, seamen or children.

Chapter Ten

MERCHANT SERVICE AND EAST INDIA COMPANY

THE RECORDS of the Merchant Service, being records of a number of private firms, are for that reason not as good as those of the Royal Navy. The various individual small companies and shipowners had no particular reason to coordinate their records until recent times, when they were required to do so under Government Acts. The records are, therefore, mainly of seamen and ships resulting from legislation brought in by governments, in order to have some control over them and information about them.

Most of these records are held by the Registrar of Shipping and Seamen, and are more accessible since they have recently been brought into the Public Record Office at Kew. Some surviving records come from a few of the Custom Offices throughout the United Kingdom. They are mainly about ships and some of the ports in question, and therefore give information on the ships themselves and their masters and owners.

Muster Rolls of merchant ships were kept from 1747. These gave the names of officers, seamen and other people employed on board, with their usual place of residence and date of joining and so forth. But unfortunately these rolls survive only for one port from 1747, namely Shields, and only for three other ports from earlier than 1800, Dartmouth, Liverpool and Plymouth.

There is a good and detailed account by Nicholas Cox of the records at the Registrar General's Office of Shipping and Seamen, published in the *Journal of Sources for Maritime History*, volume II, No. 2 (September 1972), and there is also a five-page leaflet, 'Records of the Registrar General of Shipping and Seamen', issued by the Public Record Office in 1973. This gives details of their holdings.

Crew Lists

It is unfortunate that so many of the earlier Muster Rolls have been lost. An Act of 1835 brought in the 'Agreement and Crew Lists', which required a written agreement for a man. This included the man's wages, his type of service and the nature of his voyage. These continued to 1860, but after that date, because the census returns for 1861 and onwards recorded names and details of those on board British merchant ships, they only kept a 10 per cent sample. For those seeking an ancestor who was a serving seaman, the Register of Seamen's Services will be of particular interest. An Act of 1835 provided for the first time for Registration of Seamen. The individual seaman can be traced back by the 'Alphabetical Index of Seamen' (BT119). The registers themselves give information about men in a coded form.

Masters and Mates

In 1845 the Board of Trade brought in a voluntary examination for masters and mates on foreign-going British merchant ships. This was later made compulsory under the Act of 1850, and extended in 1854 to home trading ships. These are in the Record Office under BT124 for foreign trade, and for home trade BT125 and BT126. In numerical order these give the name, place and date of birth, any registered ticket number, rank for which examined and place and date of certificate granted.

There is a useful published list by Lloyds entitled *Lloyds Captains' Register*, comprising the names and services of certificated masters of the British Mercantile Marine then afloat, compiled from the records of the Registrar General of Seamen, 1869. This is now a rare book, but there is a copy in the Society of Genealogists, London. It does not include those who, during the five years prior to its publication, had not been afloat. Otherwise it gives the full names of masters, including those who were qualified but were serving as mates, the place and date of birth, port at which they were examined, the date of the examination, and details of the ships served in since receiving their master's certificate. With the development of steam ships, examinations for the competence of engineers were started in 1862. These are in BT139. Similar certificates for skippers and mates of fishing boats were introduced in 1853. There are also registers concerning deaths, births and marriages at sea.

The East India Company Records

These records are kept at Orbit House, 197 Blackfriars Road, London SE1 8NG. They cover the records of this great company, founded in 1601 as a trading company. The company records have been described as among the finest in the world. Much work has been done in recent years towards indexing them. As early as 1771 an official was appointed by the company to take charge of records, and from that time forward they are particularly good. It is the earlier records, from before this official's appointment, that are not well indexed, but work is being concentrated on this now. The company, as a trading company, enlisted persons starting as writers. The writers' petitions begin in 1749 and, continuing until 1805, contain useful information about persons entering in that capacity, including information about the parentage and place and date of birth. From 1806 up to 1856, when the company ceased to exist, similar information can be obtained from the 70 volumes called 'Committee of College Reference', the College being the old East India Company College, now Haileybury College. There is a two-volume index covering the whole period from 1749 to 1857. Apart from the manuscript returns relating to the three main stations of Bengal, Madras, and Bombay, there were three printed volumes by Dodwell and Miles covering the period 1780 to 1838 for the three stations; the register of *Bengal Civil Servants 1790 to 1842* by H. T. Prinsep and a *Record of Services of Madras Civilians, 1741 to 1858* by C. C. Prinsep are also valuable. Then there are good records of the officers who served in the Company's army from 1790, from which date application for cadetships are recorded in a series of 147 volumes called Cadet Papers. These contain, with other details, certificates of baptism, well indexed in 10 volumes; thus the parentage of a military officer is not difficult to discover during the period 1790–1860. There are various other records giving details of officers' careers in the East Indian Company Army for the various departments of Bengal, Madras and Bombay. There are also various MS Army Lists for the 18th century and printed ones for the 19th century to 1860. Then the *East India Register* from 1803 onwards gives a list of the Army officers.

The medical services of the company have been well-covered in two published works. These are Lieut.-Col. D. G. Crawford's *History of the IMS* in two volumes, 1914, and his later work *Roll of the IMS 1615–1859*.

The company had both a navy and a merchant navy service. Genealogical details of sea officers in these services are less easy to trace than the ones in the army. There are three volumes of baptismal certificates of some officers, covering the period 1780 to 1830, mentioned in section 3 of the 'List of Marine Records', under 'Miscellaneous'. Fuller details of the marine records will be found in the *List of Marine Records of the late East India Company*, published in 1896.

One of the great glories of the East India Company records are the ships' logs, which from 1702 are fairly complete for ships coming out from England and returning there. There are also some accounts of earlier voyages from 1605. These logs often have, in separate books, lists of officers, crew and sometimes of passengers also on board. Published lists of ships' logs indicate if any lists of officers and crew survive. And then there is the pay book in which you may get your ancestor's signature for his pay. A printed list, *Register of Ships employed in the service of the Honourable the East India Company*, was compiled by Charles Hardy and published in 1798. His son, Horatio C. Hardy, compiled two supplementary volumes to bring the work down to 1812. From then onwards the *East India Register* gives similar information. There is also C. R. Lowe's *History of the India Navy 1613–1863*.

You will also find records at Orbit House of those employees commonly known as 'uncovenanted civilians' who were only available for subordinate appointments and were sometimes known as 'monthly writers'.

Since, from the earliest times of the Company until 1834, no one was allowed to go to India unless he had the Company's permission, nor could he stay there without a licence, one can trace fairly easily people who went out to India and also when they returned.

Applications would appear in the Court Minutes of the Company, and permission may be granted in these records and an announcement made in the *Despatches*. Then there were 'free merchants', who were merchants allowed to trade on their own account. These had to have securities from two people to cover £2,000. This appears in the Court Minutes of the Company. In the 18th century a list of persons in India who were not servants of the company was shown in a special series, beginning in Madras in 1702, in Bombay in 1719 and in Bengal in 1749. The *East India Register* from 1803 to 1837 contains similar lists. There are also 25 volumes for 1766–1829 covering Europeans who were not employees of the company, and who had been accused of misconduct.

There is a large series of more than 800 volumes called *Home Miscellaneous* which cover a multitude of matters. There is a detailed catalogue with a good index compiled by S. C. Hill and published by the India Office in 1927.

The ecclesiastical records of the Company have been well kept. The chaplains of the various factory stations were responsible for the churches or chapels there and had to forward to East India House in London copies of baptism, marriage and burial registers, so that even where the originals have been destroyed, as those of St Anne's, Calcutta, were during the time of the Black Hole and Siege, certified copies are available. A great deal has been done in recent times to index names of persons, baptised, married and buried in India, and therefore it is not difficult to discover such information. Apart from this, a great number of the registers have been published, and also many of the inscriptions on European tombs in India have been published. Wills and inventories of East India Company servants are sometimes recorded in the *Consultations*. There are, for instance, a number of copies of 18th-century wills in the St Helena *Consultations*. Other wills have been recorded in the Mayors' Courts of the various settlements and there is now a manuscript alphabetical index of wills and administrations covered by these courts for the following years; Bengal 1704–79, Madras 1753–79, Bombay 1728–83. There is also a register of all the wills proved in the three presidencies for the following years: Bengal from 1728, Madras from 1736, and Bombay from 1723 onwards.

The National Army Museum in London also has much information about East India Company officers. This includes the Hobson index, which is complete for officers of the armies, maritime services and civil services of the Bengal, Madras and Bombay presidencies. E. N. A. Baxter's *Brief Guide to Biographical Sources*, published in 1979, is a useful guide to the many sources of biographical interest scattered among the India Office library and records.

More detailed information about the records of professional men, lawyers, doctors and also of men who served in the army, navy or merchant service or East India Company will be found in my book *In Search of Ancestry* (4th edition, 1983).

Chapter Eleven

THE NATIONAL LIBRARY OF WALES

WELSH PEOPLE tracing their family history are fortunate in the existence of the National Library of Wales, where so many essential records are available. The Library was first incorporated by charter granted by King Edward VII in 1907. In 1911 the foundation stones of the permanent building were laid by King George V and Queen Mary, the following year the Library received under the Copyright Act of 1911 the right to receive a copy of all books published in Great Britain, and in 1926 it was approved by the Master of the Rolls as a depository for manorial records.

Since then approval for various numbers and types of records have been made. In 1934 the archives of the Presbyterian Church of Wales were deposited in the Library, and in 1944 the records of the Church in Wales were deposited. A further step was taken in 1945 when the ecclesiastical probate records were transferred from the District Probate Offices in Wales together with sealed copies of the instruments of tithe apportionment, then in the custody of the Welsh Church Commission or their agents, under the instructions and directions of the Master of the Rolls.

In 1955 the Central Hall was finished and Queen Elizabeth II officially opened the building. Then in 1960 the Library was appointed as a depository for a number of records held under the Public Records Act of 1958. Two years later, in 1962, the Records of the Courts of Great Session, 1742 to 1830, were transferred from the Public Record Office in London, and in 1969 the Second Bookstack Building was begun, covering the ground and first floor in Phase I, and this was completed in 1972. In 1978 the building of the Second Bookstack under Phase II was begun and was completed in 1980.

Already a number of projects have been completed, perhaps the most important being a volume by the library for later publication, in co-operation with the county record offices in Wales, containing details of original parish registers, the bishops' transcripts, microfilm copies, facsimiles and other copies held by other record depositories in Wales. The library also holds various publications of the Society of Genealogists.

The Department of Manuscripts has a useful eight-page pamphlet *A Guide to Genealogical Sources of the National Library of Wales*, briefly giving main sources. A fuller edition of this is now being compiled and will be available to readers in due course.

Probate Records

The early probate registers up to 1858, which were under the control of the Church and have now been handed over to the National Library, are in the process of being indexed. Those of the Bangor Consistory Court, volume 1, pre-1700, have already been published, and the library intends to publish further index volumes. The Archdeaconry Court of Brechin up to 1660 is likely to be the next volume.

Then the probate records both before and since the civil registration of wills and administration, which took the place of the church in 1858 onwards, are gradually being entered on card indexes. That for Bangor Probate Records, 1858 to 1930, has already been compiled and the Carmarthen Probate Records, 1824 to 1841, which has no MS index available, is also being taken in hand.

Nonconformist Records

Typescript catalogues of nonconformist records in the library are available. These include a substantial holding relating to the Calvinistic Methodists, otherwise known as the Presbyterian Church of Wales, and the Wesleyan Methodists.

Monumental Inscriptions

These inscriptions, which are such an asset to genealogists, are covered by the *Handlist of Manuscripts in the National Library of Wales*. It is important to note that the MSS often contain only copies of selected inscriptions, but the various family history societies now established in Wales are making systematic recordings, usually covering all monumental inscriptions to and sometimes beyond 1837, and will almost certainly deposit copies in the National Library.

The pamphlet on Genealogical Sources in the Library points out that it is not intended to take the place of professional work, and does not attempt to give a detailed description of sources and procedure, suggesting for these one of the general guides to genealogy, such as Anthony Camp's *Tracing Your Ancestors* (1970), Gerald Hamilton-Edwards, *In Search of Ancestry* (1974) and Arthur J. Willis, *Genealogy for Beginners* (1970). The two latter works have more recent editions, *In Search of Ancestry* in 1983, and *Genealogy for Beginners* (A.J.W. with M. Tatchell) in 1984.

The guide points out that genealogical resources in the library are not only in the Department of MSS and Records, since much material, such as electoral lists, newspapers and directories, in the Department of Printed Books, which are often of great value in compiling a family history, and such items as plans and sale catalogues, in the Department of Prints, Drawings and Maps, may also be found useful.

Before going into the library searchers should arrange all the information they have already got together, and make a summary of this information obtained in accordance with the instructions in previous chapters. It is useful to have the facts at one's finger tips – such matters as the results of research in the General Register Office in London, or at the County Record Offices and Census Returns. A chart pedigree is a good way of putting together succinctly the information so far attained, with notes on the names in the pedigree on a separate sheet. Differences in Welsh sources have been pointed out in previous chapters, such as the later adoption of surnames in Wales through the continuance of patronymics until the 17th century, and in the country areas even up to the 19th century.

The pamphlet gives examples of the way in which this use of patronymics so much later than in England can appear confusing. It mentions as an example that Griffith Lewis was the son of John William; that Harry David was the son of David John Rees, these both being witnesses to a grant of property in the parish of Llandeilo Fawr, Carmarthenshire, in 1683; and that the marriage of Thomas Morris and Elizabeth Morris, spinster, son and daughter of Morris Thomas, farmer, are recorded in the parish register of Llansilin, Denbyshire, exactly a century later.

Parish Registers

Of the parish registers of the Church in Wales, that is of the Anglican Church in Wales, registers from some 400 or more parishes have already been deposited in the National Library, and further copies are continually being added. Some registers are also being deposited in local record offices since they have been established. A great number of registers, however, are still in the custody of the incumbents of parishes.

The publication by Mrs. J. A. Tallis, *Original Parish Registers in Record Offices and Libraries*, published by the Local Population Studies Society in 1974, is very useful. It must be remembered that a number of parish priests are continually transferring their early registers for safe custody to record offices. Already a first supplement to this work has been made by Miss E. O. Peach (1976). In the National Library itself there is a complete list of deposited registers, which are arranged alphabetically for each diocese, and this can be consulted in the Reading Room for the Department of Manuscripts.

While the order for keeping parish registers came into being in 1538, the earliest surviving registers in Wales do not begin before about 1660 and even then the starting dates vary considerably.

Bishops' Transcripts

These were not as regularly sent in as they should have been, and others have been lost or have seriously deteriorated. There are no transcripts before 1662 deposited in the library, and after that date there are many gaps. There are only a few transcripts before 1723 in the diocese of Llandaff, and hardly any for the 18th-century parishes in the Archdeaconry of Cardigan in St David's diocese.

These transcripts cease at various dates in the 19th century. By 1837 Civil Registration had been introduced, and this made transcripts less important than previously. Schedules are available for the bishops' transcripts held in the Department of Manuscripts.

Marriage Licences

Marriage Allegations and Bonds, necessary to obtain a licence, which enabled a person to marry without having banns called publicly in the parish church three Sundays before the marriage ceremony, mainly cover the 18th and 19th centuries and the first 30 years of the 20th century. The amount of information in these documents varies with the different dioceses: marriage bonds are the most useful source for family historians. Although marriage licences were used more frequently than is usually imagined and were by no means confined to the upper classes, probably fewer than one in ten people obtained marriage licences.

Information on Clergy

Various church records in the library will give you such information. Among the most important sources are ordination papers, particularly when the person concerned is not a university graduate. The papers should contain a baptismal certificate for the person being ordained.

Again, it should be remembered that the Nonconformist records in the library are far less extensive than the volumes and papers of the Anglican Church in Wales. These records have been discussed more fully in Chapter Six.

Probate Records

The wills proved and administrations granted in the ecclesiastical court prior to 1858 have been deposited in the National Library of Wales, and these have been more fully discussed in Chapter Seven. Further details regarding these records will be found in A. J. Camp's *Wills and their Whereabouts* (1974) and in J. S. W. Gibson's *A Simplified Guide to Probate Jurisdictions* (2nd edn., 1983).

The probate records held in the library cover the whole of Wales, with the exception of 15 of the border parishes in the diocese of Hereford. There are also 17 English parishes which came under Welsh jurisdiction and have been included. But the probate records of the diocese (including peculiar courts) of Hereford, which were formerly in the National Library, have been transferred to the Hereford Record Office.

There are MSS calendars or indexes available for a majority of the probate records in the library.

One complication concerning indexes is that, because the Welsh continued much later than the English to use patronymics, earlier indexes are arranged either chronologically or, as in the case of St Asaph, in alphabetical order under Christian names. However, a surnames index for St Asaph has been compiled for 1729 to 1820, and similar card indexes are being prepared for other periods.

This chapter will, I hope, give you a good idea of the vast amount of material in the National Library to assist you in your search for your family history. There is also here a great quantity of family documents for various families, and heraldic documents of families entitled to bear arms. These are referred to in subsequent chapters.

A Welsh dragon holding in his dexter paw a scroll, from the Armorial Bearings granted to the National Library of Wales.

Chapter Twelve

MANOR COURT, CHANCERY AND OTHER RECORDS

Tithe Records and Maps

UNDER THE apportionment schedules, implemented by the Tithe Commutation Act of 1836, tithe maps covering the whole of Wales are available and are most valuable in fixing the location of estates and farms. The maps are reasonably detailed to a large scale, and record the names of owners or occupiers at that date. Originally tithes were levied to support the church but in early times, even before the Reformation, tithe income had been transferred for the use of various bodies, both clerical and lay. Accounts were kept by the recipients of tithes of their livestock and crops, or, in other cases, money received in lieu of these. Some account books have survived among estate records, and they record names of persons paying the tithes and the date at which they ceased to do so, a useful fact to have, possibly indicating the date the payer died. These Welsh tithe records are held in the National Library of Wales.

Estate and Personal Papers

There are collections of deeds, correspondence, accounts and rentals and so forth in the National Library and several have been catalogued in some detail, with TS schedules. As with the tithes, rentals can be useful, not least for indicating when a person died. These collections are in the MS Department, where there is a suitable card index to the TS schedules. Sections in the indexes indicate wills, marriage settlements, inquisitions post-mortem and any pedigrees. If you are searching the estate of a person in whom you have particular interest, this will tell you a great deal about him and his family. Otherwise the personal name index may not help you particularly, as it is a selective one and will not usually include, for instance, the names of parties to deeds. It will probably include only references to fairly well-known persons, and possibly recipients and writers of some of the letters. The topographical index, on the other hand, is more comprehensive and may refer to individuals once you know where they were living.

There is an explanatory introduction to the index and to schedules in the Reading Room of the department.

The index to the general MSS in the library has been partly published in the *Handlist of Manuscripts in the National Library of Wales.*

Manor Court Records

One of the useful sources in tracing your pedigree back earlier than the parish registers is the Manorial Record.

Manorial Rolls are often still in private hands and, apart from the difficulty in tracing who owns them, the chances of their survival are not too great. Many of those surviving are registered in the Historical MSS Commission, Manor Documents Register, Quality House, Quality Court, Chancery Lane, London, WC2. Today, legislation guards against manorial records being destroyed or sold overseas.

If you should be able to discover manorial rolls covering the parish or parishes in which you are interested, you may learn a great deal about your ancestors and succeed in tracing them, even though they might have been only humble people.

In the manor court rolls all copyholders' deeds are recorded, such as marriage settlements or mortgages of an estate. Juries assembed after the death of a tenant of the Lord of the Manor and recorded their investigations into what estate the tenant died possessed, the name and relationship of his heir and what fine or heriot was due to the lord.

These 'presentments', as they were called, often included extracts from the deceased's will or other deeds. John West's *Village Records* (Phillimore, 1982) gives good information on manorial records, with facsimiles and transcripts of documents. The National Library's holdings of manorial records is most complete for the county of Montgomery. Some of these manorial records relating to Wales may be in the Public Record Office in Chancery Lane, London, and details of such holdings will be found in the two volumes of the *Guide to the Public Record Office* (1963 and 1968). A useful book in tracing material at the Public Record Office in London or at Kew is *Tracing Your Ancestors in the Public Record Office* (1981) by Jane Cox and Timothy Padfield.

More and more surviving manorial records are coming to the notice of the Manorial Register each year.

Chancery Records

Chancery proceedings can also be of high importance. It has been said that few land-owning families have gone through their history without some dispute in the Chancery Court. Such a case, if it is discovered, can reveal a wealth of information and relationships. The case papers may include pedigrees, particularly likely among the Master's Papers. One advantage of Chancery cases is that the whole evidence was conducted in writing, so that you can follow the case in detail. Certificates of baptism, extracts of deeds, wills and other documents from the family muniment room may also be discovered among the evidence produced.

The proceedings in Chancery cases are by Bill of Complaint, which is in the form of a petition to the Lord Chancellor, Lord Keeper or the Lords Commissioners of the Great Seal. This is followed by the Answer, and the evidence is given by means of affidavits, depositions, then further questions arising from the answers, and so on. These are all there to be read. Thus the whole story is told on paper and you have the advantage of being able to read all the evidence considered by the court at the time. Chancery proceedings are preserved in the Public Record Office in London.

One of the difficulties in using chancery proceedings is in discovering what exists. Apart from some of the very early proceedings, there are no printed calendars, and the MS calendars in the PRO are divided among the six clerks in chancery – the 'prothonotaries' as they are called – and run concurrently. Therefore it is necessary to search for each year in six different places. In addition it is sometimes difficult to identify a particular case, for the calendar or index will merely say 'Smith v. Jones', or whatever the names are. This may not be too difficult if you are searching a rare surname, but where the name is common, then the process of searching is onerous and lengthy. Such a search could only be undertaken if you were greatly depending on the result of it.

However, sometimes there is mention of a chancery suit in a will, which will definitely let you know that there was such a suit and give some idea of the date at which it is likely to have been held. Another possible clue is a mention on the back of a deed connected with one of the people concerned, showing that it was produced in some chancery case, as solicitors have a habit of making such notes and sometimes give the actual reference of the case.

There is a very good little booklet which explains these proceedings, by R. F. E. Garrett, called *Chancery and other Proceedings*, originally published in the *Genealogists' Magazine* as articles in September and December 1965, and later issued as a booklet by Malcolm Pinhorn. Then at the Society of Genealogists in London there is the Bernau Index, which is quite extensive and refers mainly to 18th-century chancery proceedings and how to track them down, but this index only covers two of the six clerks, namely Whittington-Sewell and Purcas-Winter, and unfortunately, for the other four clerks, there is no key in the calendars.

Another article in the *Genealogists' Magazine* (June 1979) by E. W. Coldham, called 'Genealogical Resources in Chancery Records', is based on a lecture given by him and gives further information about the kind of genealogical information you may find in chancery proceedings. The author's own article in the *Genealogists' Magazine* of March 1969 called 'Should Fanny have been sent to France' may also give readers some idea of the variety of information which can be discovered in one of these chancery proceedings.

Pedigree Books

These books exist in considerable number in the National Library. There is a comprehensive survey of them by Major Francis Jones, in an article entitled 'An Approach to Welsh Genealogy' in the *Transactions of the Honourable Society of Cymmrodorion* for 1948 (pp. 303–466). There are also useful printed works which will direct a searcher who is interested in Gentry Families. These are Percy C. Bartram, *Welsh Genealogies A.D. 300–1400* (1974) and

Welsh Genealogies A.D. 1400–1500,18 volumes (1983); Lewys Dwnn (ed. S. R. Meyrick), *Heraldic Visitations of Wales . . .* (1846); Thomas Nicholas, *Annals . . . of the . . . County Families of Wales* (1872); J. E. Griffith, *Pedigrees of Anglesey and Carnarvonshire Families* (1914); G. T. Clark, *Limbus Patrum Morganiae et Glamorganiae* (1886). J. Y. W. Lloyd, *History of . . . Powys Fadog* (1881–7), and *West Wales Historical Records* (1922–29).

Naturally any particular families, the pedigrees of which are discovered by you in the library, may prove valuable. Also naturally these pedigrees vary considerably in the amount of information they give. Some may be of the nobility of the later middle ages, which have continued to be copied and added to by later generations. They may, on the other hand, simply be charts, the work of amateurs who have given their copies of them to the library. The earlier types mentioned may not reach back before the end of the 17th century, while the more amateur pedigrees may, on the other hand, be much more recent ones. The difficult period is about the end of the 17th and the beginning of the 18th century.

Some collections of pedigrees, such as the Pedigree Books of Alewyn C. Evans of Carmarthen, are in the National Library MSS department, and a great number of early pedigrees may be found in the Peniarth Collection. Another collection of important volumes of pedigrees came from Wynnstay, and a copy of the collection known as the 'Golden Grove Book' is now in the Carmarthen Record Office with the Castell Gorfod collection.

The National Library also has a great number of other deeds and documents, some of which are calendared in volume I, *The Coleman Deeds*, which were compiled by Francis Green, editor of *West Wales Historical Records* (Aberystwyth, 1921). This volume is not indexed. These deeds cover a great many interesting items, such as, for instance, a grant dated 1 October 1549 'by Philip ap David ap Ieuan ap Llewelin of Llannell, near Craghoell, co. Brecnon, yeoman, to John ap Ieuan ap John of a cottage with its appurtenances, to wit, in length from the Meadow of the aforesaid Philip to the Lord's waste there, and in breath [*sic*], from the land of Hoell ap Jenkin called *Crayoke ye Keefab* to the land of Hoell ap Hoell *etc.*'

Another deed, in volume 3 (indexed) of a Calendar of Deeds and Documents of the Hawarden Deeds, compiled by Francis Green . . . Aberystwith, National Library of Wales (Cardiff . . . 1931), refers (fr. 1305/s 1333, 1915), to 'Catherine da. of Sir Stephen Glynne, 8th Bart., and wife of the Rt. Hon. W. E. Gladstone 1895–6' (1914–15). This is, of course, the wife of the famous Victorian Prime Minister.

Some dispute resulting in a Chancery case.

Chapter Thirteen

LANDED AND ARMIGEROUS FAMILIES

THE LAW RELATING to arms in England and Wales is quite clear and straightforward. A person, to be entitled to use armorial bearings, must satisfy one of three conditions; he must either descend in the male line from a person to whom arms have been granted and recorded at the College of Arms, London, or be able to prove descent in the male line from a person who has been recognised as armigerous in a Visitation by a member of the college, or (thirdly) have obtained a grant of arms to himself. If you have an idea that you are entitled to use arms, you should find this out by approaching an officer of the College of Arms who will investigate this possibility for a reasonable fee. You will need to give him the descent of your ancestors as far as you have discovered it, and also supply the evidence to support your discoveries.

If it should be proved that you have a right to arms from an earlier ancestor, then this will also bring you information about your forbears. If the result of these enquiries is negative, then you can still consider applying for a grant to yourself. This will cost you fees which have in recent years considerably increased because of inflation.

As with other Celtic races living in mountainous country racial identity was strong, and the habits of centuries were not easily discarded. The Welsh, like the Scots, were noted for a great love of heraldry and genealogy. Many old pedigrees, stretching far back, could be recited from memory.

Even so a great many Welsh pedigrees have been recorded and it is interesting to note that up to 1804 as many as 7,773 had been registered at the College of Arms, London. Presumably most, if not all, were of armigerous families.

It has been noted that Welsh families, as with other races, which lived in the more remote country districts had usually continued as landed owners for generations, while those which had lived nearer to the towns tended to possess lands which had changed hands a number of times, or had been dispersed. This has been mentioned in an essay by Sir John Habakkuk on 'Marriage and the Ownership of Land' in *Welsh Society and Nationhood, Historical Essays presented to Glanlor Williams*, p. 178, edited by R. R. Davies and others (Cardiff, University of Wales Press, 1984).

Habakkuk writes:

> In one of his few references to Wales in *The Wealth of Nations* Adam Smith makes an interesting observation: 'Very old families, such as have possessed some considerable estate from father to son for many successive generations, are very rare in commercial countries. In countries which have little commerce, on the contrary, such as Wales or the Highlands of Scotland, they are very common.'

One of the difficulties with Welsh pedigrees that have been recorded from memory is that dates are seldom mentioned and family homes are not always named. Some pedigrees recorded in this way are of fantastic length and Guttun Owain, in one case, traces an Elizabethan landlord to 'Adam, son of God'!

People adopting arms to which they had no right.

Chapter Fourteen

DEVELOPMENT OF FAMILY HISTORY

IN RECENT YEARS there has been a tremendous interest in tracing family history, and also in developing the history beyond a mere pedigree. Some family histories of the past have just recorded brief details about the family, which has not made for interesting reading. In recent years people have made the point that a family history should place some emphasis on historical background, giving information, for instance, about how topical events may have influenced the movements and occupations of one's ancestors. In dealing with a person's occupation or trade a description of the kind of work when the ancestor lived has added great interest to the family history. For an example, Donald Steel, in his *Discovering your Family History* (1980), gives details of the work and conditions of a sawyer at Plymouth Dockyard in the early 19th century, and my last chapter in this book tries to show how much more interesting a family history can be made by infusing some historical background and local influences into the account.

The wave of interest in family history is probably due to a number of causes. Sometimes service during a war may have sparked this off. A young son gets called up into a regiment and the family begin talking about the regiment in which he has been called to serve. 'Has anyone else in the family ever served in that regiment?', one will ask and then perhaps the grandfather or great-uncle will say 'Yes. I believe my grandfather served in it', and then there will be a general discussion in the family about it. They will probably ask the grandfather the name of his grandfather, and then you will be getting back to a great-great-grandfather of the younger generation. Perhaps the elderly relative will not be able to remember the name of the regiment, but will remember he was called a 'Fusilier'. 'Why Fusilier and not Private?' Then Uncle Idris, who prides himself about his knowledge of the army and its regiments, will contribute 'Fusilier! That limits the possible regiments.' He should have gone into the 23rd or Welch Fusiliers, as a Welshman, but then the army does not always do the obvious thing. He might have gone into the Northumberland or Lancashire Fusiliers, or even into the Scots Fusiliers. Anyway that limited the regiments, and the muster rolls of the regiments could be consulted and that would show which one, and should tell us where he was born.

Then he might have served in the Royal Navy and in that case it will be necessary to track down in which ship or ships he served. Perhaps an old cap ribbon may be found, and this will tell you straightaway, or his discharge papers would tell you even more. That will lead to information about him and his birthplace from the muster rolls of the ships in which he served.

Another reason why people have become interested in their forbears is that the possibilities of discovering something about them are much greater today with the increased accessibility of records. The institution of county record offices, where a great deal of material has been accumulated and is available, helps considerably in your search. Here you will probably find the earlier registers of the parishes in which your ancestors may have been baptised, married or buried, and possibly ancestral wills.

Then in the Public Record Office a good deal of new material has become available. An example of this is the records of the Merchant Service. It is easier, now that these records have been transferred to the PRO, to trace information about a forbear who was a merchant seaman. Then there has been a great deal of indexing of wills and administrations, much of which has been published by the Index Society. All this has led to people thinking about their ancestors and forming themselves into societies to meet and benefit from the experience of others interested in this pursuit. These societies have lectures on the various methods of going about ancestry tracing.

In 1974 the Federation of Family History Societies was formed to co-ordinate the activities of all these societies, and most, if not all, such societies have become members of it, as have a number of other societies with an interest in family history. These include the Society of Genealogists in London, the Heraldry Society, The Institute of Heraldic and Genealogical Studies in Canterbury, the Devon and Cornwall Record Society, the Scottish Genealogy Society and a number from the Commonwealth (nine from Australia) and the United States of America. By March 1982 there was a family history society covering every county in England. A few covered two counties, such as Somerset and Dorset, while some have two such societies, for instance, Cheshire and North Cheshire, Kent and North-West Kent, Central, North and West Middlesex, East and West Surrey, East Yorkshire and York societies. There are even societies covering one particular place and its neighbourhood, such as the Folkestone Society. Seven societies in England have a membership of over a thousand. The Federation publishes a quarterly journal *Family History News and Digest* and a number of special publications from time to time, such as *Marriage Indexes, Aids for Genealogists* and *Census Returns* (1841–1871, on microfilm). Those wishing to obtain any of the publications will find the name of the Secretary among the Useful Addresses in Appendix C.

In Wales, as in Scotland, with its sparsely populated areas, the development of family history societies on a county basis has been more difficult, but it is now going ahead well, and the growth tends to be in the greater populated areas and large towns. Wales today has six family history societies: the Clwyd Family History Society covering Denbigh and Flint with a small part of Merionethshire; the Dyfed Family History Society in Cardiganshire, Carmarthenshire and Pembrokeshire; the Gwent Family History Society in Monmouthshire; the Gwynedd Family History Society, covering Anglesey, Caernarfonshire and the major part of

Merionethshire; the Powys Family History Society, covering Breconshire, Montgomeryshire and Radnorshire; and the South Wales Family History Society, covering Glamorganshire and the surrounding areas.

In addition there are two 'over-all' family societies, co-ordinating those in Wales. The 'County Family History Societies in Wales' was founded with the idea of bringing together, encouraging and helping people interested in family history in their particular county, and the 'Association of Family History Societies of Wales' was founded in March 1981 as a co-ordinating body which promotes and fosters the study of family history throughout Wales. Meeting twice a year, it makes representations to official bodies on any matters affecting family history research in Wales.

The local Welsh family history societies have the same aims as those in England and Scotland. They hold monthly meetings which include talks on family history subjects, particularly directed towards helping people in a practical way with sources which they should use. The societies also occasionally make visits elsewhere of genealogical value, and any visitors, from overseas particularly, are sure of a welcome if they care to attend a meeting.

One of the most important functions at these family history societies is local research. This includes transcribing registers and, in local graveyards, monumental inscriptions, at any rate up to 1837 (when the civil registration began) and possibly a bit further. All these societies publish journals two or three times a year, with space for queries and problems from members, and also articles of family history and local interest.

It is not only local members who join these societies. Persons overseas may join the family history society of the area from which their ancestors came. Such members will exchange information with other family historians.

Chapter Fifteen

YOUR OWN FAMILY HISTORY

DO NOT PUT OFF writing it up until you think you have collected everything. In family history there is no such thing as having reached the end. People put off writing up the material they have accumulated, which may be a considerable amount, because they think they must round it off. This will never happen. So determine to write up what you have found out so far, when you feel with reason you have accumulated a fair quantity, so that future descendants will have the benefit of your work. If you do not do this, you will merely have given yourself some enjoyment and satisfaction in tracing your family so far and then your research will be lost and wasted.

One of the advantages of the formation of One-Name Societies, which are growing considerably every year, is that a number of people interested in the same surname work together, taking down information from a variety of records, one perhaps doing parish registers of a certain locality for a particular period, another extracting wills of a certain area, perhaps the archdeaconry wills and administrations there, or the consistory court, or both. This, of course, can only be done with a name which is fairly rare, and a name covering people who have a surname linked with a certain place or district; for there is, of course, no particular reason why people with a surname from some trade, or from a nickname, should have any relationship with each other.

If, however, you have such a name which suggests relationship, such as one from a certain place or prevalent in a particular area, then you will help others in your work and also benefit from their work on the surname of your own particular interest.

In any case it is important that you should leave some clear record of the work you have done on your family, so that future generations may benefit from it. How often people say 'If only I had asked my grandfather when I was young! What a lot he could have told me!' This is absolutely true, and what a pity you did not do so!

However this is something that nearly everybody had regretted. Another point is that so often people have done a considerable amount of work on the family, but their efforts, perhaps in some notebook or even in a typescript, have been thrown away by later generations.

Remember also that in writing up your family history you are making a small contribution to social history; each family differs from the next, sometimes quite considerably, and the conditions of life of each generation – the sort of occupations or trades they took up, how their social standard may have risen or fallen – these are all fascinating matters which can delight and intrigue social historians.

Another matter you must consider is how you will preserve your work. It is not good enough to leave it to a nephew or great-nephew, whom you decide is interested in the family history and will look after it, perhaps add to it, and then pass it on in his turn to a descendant in the next generation, whom he thinks will do likewise, praiseworthy though this is. You must also think how you can leave a copy of the history where it will be preserved by some continuing body or society. For example, the catalogue of the British Museum Library, now the British Library, reveals the existence of many pedigrees, reproduced by some process, such as xerox or die-line. This library is usually willing to take straightforward pedigrees, which are drawn-up clearly, because such a pedigree takes up very little room and it would probably be kept until it can be bound up with a number of others, forming a book of pedigrees. Each pedigree would be catalogued under the name of the family as well as under the compiler of the pedigree (if his or her name is clearly shown on the pedigree, preferably with an address).You should also send a copy of the pedigree to prominent members of the family, to your county record office and to the main library in your area and in the area to which the family belonged.

Of course, another advantage of producing an account of the family is that you will stimulate the family's interest, and you may get some of them sending in corrections: uncles or aunts may write indignantly saying, 'Great Uncle Owen was never in the 23rd Welsh Fusiliers, it was the 47th, of course'. Or else they may correct some name or let you know one of them was always known as 'Snoggy', perhaps telling you why!

I have suggested earlier in this book, and in my *In Search of Ancestry* and *In Search of Scottish Ancestry*, the best ways of recording your family. The record in chart form is one of the simplest and clearest ways of showing the various generations of the family and giving a little information about them. You need such a pedigree, anyway, even if you are going to write up a fuller account. There is no doubt that a chart pedigree shows the ancestry in a simple way, though it is nevertheless a skilful job. I myself try to deal first with those lines which have no descent or descent in which one is not personally interested, and then to continue with the main lines which carries on the pedigree, or that part of it I wish to carry on. If you study pedigrees in other genealogical books, this will help you. Examples of good chart pedigrees, with a great deal of detail, are Crisp's *Visitations*, which are a modern way of recording details, such as those given in the Herald's Visitation, containing not so much information as to overburden and therefore confuse, the pedigree. Other examples of good chart pedigrees are in Cussans' *History of Hertfordshire* and Ormerod's *History of the County and City of Cheshire*. Although both these were published in the last century, the pedigrees they include are good examples of layout, and of the amount of detail you can include without destroying the clarity of the chart.

There are, however, examples of pedigrees in historical or biographical works which are deplorably lacking in detail and sometimes in clarity. My own pedigrees in *In Search of Ancestry* and *In Search of Scottish Ancestry*, as well as in this book, follow the pattern I have devised. You must be consistent with abbreviations, and not use the same abbreviation for two types of words. For instance keep 'b' for born and 'bap.' for baptised, 'bur.' for buried. You can use 'm' for married and 'd.' for died. Other abbreviations you can see in the pedigrees in my own books. Christian names should be in full, and I prefer to give surnames with every male entry, though females are not given the surname, as these change on marriage.

Information can be extended to a chart pedigree by giving notes on some of the entries, as required. These are best as capital letters alongside the person's name, and the notes can be carried on separate pages and be as brief or lengthy as required. This can give a great deal of information about individuals without destroying the clarity of the pedigree itself. I have very brief notes on individuals in my pedigree 'Mainly from Registers of Deeds', in *In Search of Scottish Ancestry* (pp. 106–7), but these brief entries could have been increased considerably and shown on a separate page.

The type of pedigree used in such publications as *Burke's Peerage* and *Burke's Landed Gentry*, is known as a Tabular Pedigree. These should be studied. Such a form of pedigree can quite easily be reproduced by xerox after being typed. If you needed 40 or 50 copies, this can be made up into quite an attractive small booklet, by having it set and reduced to A5 page size, from A4, and printed back and front, thus getting four pages on each sheet of A4 paper, as I have done with some of my booklets, such as *Perthshire Marriage Contracts*. The pages can be stapled together with a suitable cover and be made quite presentable. A number of firms do this sort of work, some of whom specialise in work for architects for their plans, and for other societies for their annual reports. These are all reproduced from typewriting. In fact, today many books are produced from some process of sophisticated typewriting.

You will notice that in this kind of pedigree it is necessary to continue the pedigree down one line, by using the words 'of whom presently' against the person through whom you have decided to continue the line. This would sometimes be the elder line, but not necessarily so. In the past, with the *Landed Gentry*, the lands usually descended through the eldest son, or a peerage normally went through the eldest son or other male heir. But through whatever line you decide to take your pedigree, you must try to exhaust the descendants of all the other members of the family as you come to them. With a pedigree starting far back, this sometimes means continuing for many generations, each indented, so that the page is indented further and further, until you almost reach the half-way division. For this reason you cannot give too much detail for each person, or otherwise it would go on for several pages and become confusing. This is demonstrated in some of the cases of older families in the *Peerage* or *Landed Gentry*. An example from the peerage of many younger branches is that of the Earls of Huntingdon, and a family in the *Landed Gentry* which is well-extended to many generations is that of Giffard. If you study these and other such pedigrees you will soon learn how the matter is handled.

THE WHITTOW FAMILY

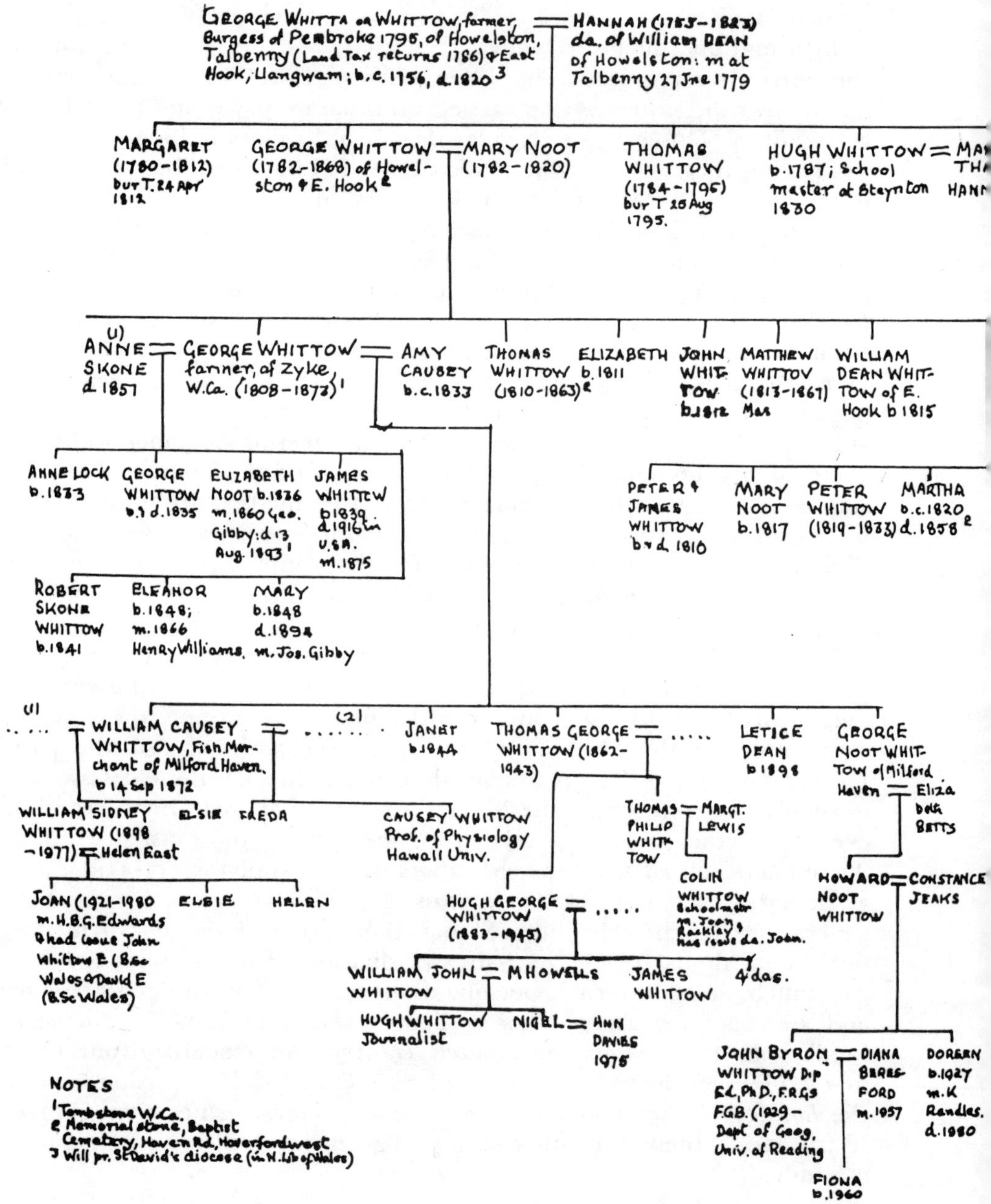

OF PEMBROKESHIRE

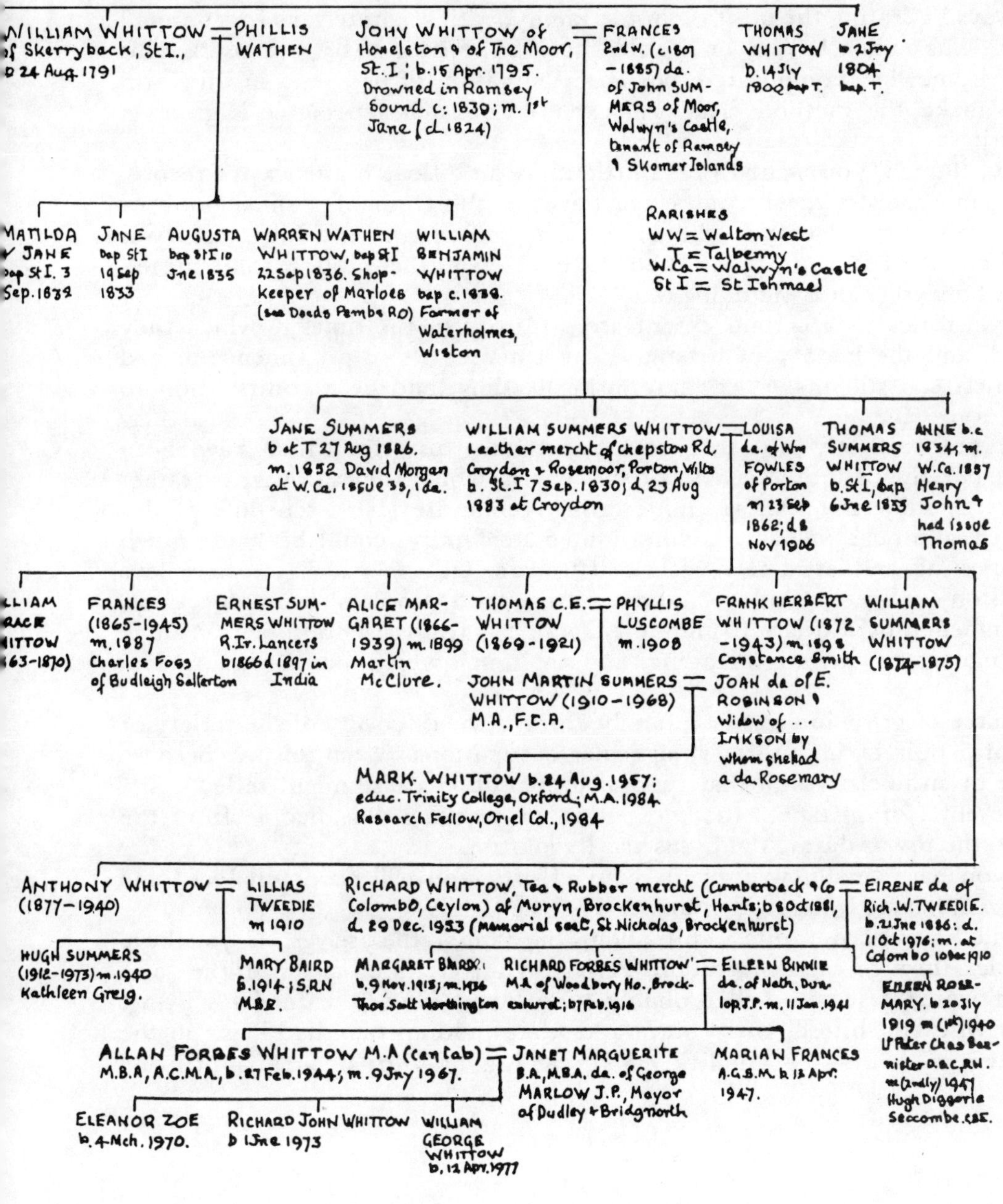

One important point in recording tabular pedigrees is the numerical notation of each member of the family. This shows to which generation he or she belongs. One way of doing this with typewriting is to use a mixture of roman and arabic figures, both upper and lower case, possibly in this order: I, 1, (1), (i). A slight disadvantage in using roman figures is that they have various spacings, i.e. I, II, III, IV, and so on. This need not be of any consequence so long as you keep the indentation even, regardless of the number of spaces which the roman figures take up. Other people may prefer to use arabic figures throughout, which, under 10, remain single spaced. In any case, after about four generations indented, you have to continue with additional symbols, which are best in the form of 1a, 2a, 3a, and then the children of those so marked will be, 1b, 2b, 3b, and so on, the figure always indicating the position in the family, with separate runs for sons and daughters. Thus a male 1b may be the eldest son of perhaps 1a or perhaps 2a. This may seem somewhat complicated, but an examination of pedigrees in this form will soon make the method clear. An example of such a pedigree is given in Appendix B.

Possibly, though, you want to be a little more ambitious in the way of recording your family history, with more narrative, in the form of a small book or booklet. In the first place you should not imagine that your family history is going to be dull. It is up to you not to make it so, and there follow some suggestions as to how you can avoid doing this.

Family histories to a certain extent are a history of the times in which they were lived, and the history of a family which never rose to prominence or had high position can still make very interesting reading, and be a contribution to social history.

This is unfortunately not true of many family histories which have been produced, but this is more because of the way in which they are written rather than that the subject matter is uninteresting. Some are just a schedule of dry facts which, although valuable to the immediate family, could be made much more interesting and attractive with a little care. Others, which try to relieve the monotony of such dull recitation, often tend towards being facetious, possibly impelled by a desire for modesty, which is really a false modesty. Such accounts make very irritating reading, and are much worse than a mere factual account.

One source of great interest in a family story is the discovery of the variety of reasons for people taking up their particular occupations. Often this was because the father or an uncle was in that type of job; another cause might reflect some national event, for instance, the movement of working-class people from the country to the towns during the Industrial Revolution.

When you have finally written up your efforts, you will no doubt feel some satisfaction in having concluded your work on the family.

You will have learnt quite a bit about the family themselves, as you have worked back through each generation. Perhaps your grandfather was in the 1881 census, in which case you will probably have learnt how he earned his living, where his wife and himself were born, and what children they had living in the house: there is always a possibility that there was an aunt or great-aunt living there and this fact alone will take you back a number of generations, because it will give her birthplace, and link the family up with this place. Then, as you have got back further, earlier census returns and family wills may have provided more details of the kind of life led by your forbears, and to a certain extent whether they did well in their careers or not. You will certainly know very much more about them than you ever thought possible and will have enjoyed noticing the development and progress of their lives.

All this information, of course, you will be leaving for the descendants of the family. Make sure you have made a number of copies of your account and deposit them in your local record office, or the record office of the area to which the family belonged, and likewise the local library and possibly the British Library, which is often willing to accept family histories, or even chart pedigrees. In that case they will be entered in the catalogue under the family name. Similarly the National Library of Wales will be interested in a copy of your work. All this helps to make sure that anyone in the future can find out if anything has been written about the family either through the British Library Catalogue, or through other catalogues. In this way you will make sure your work had not been in vain, you can feel you have done your duty and be satisfied that you have left a record of your forbears for posterity.

APPENDIX A

Suggested Questionnaire for sending out to the family. The general queries may apply to most families, but more detailed enquiries will, of course, vary greatly in different cases. Plenty of room should be left after each question for the replies.

General Questions
Do you know of the existence of any of the following, relating to earlier members of the family:

Family Bible, giving dates of baptism, marriage, burial etc.
Family pedigree or written account or notes of the family.
Any copies of wills, any diaries, note books, birthday books, old receipt books, account books, tontine or stock and share certificates, old deeds relating to property, estate maps, bank books, life assurance policies, apprenticeship indentures, family samplers, funeral cards or bookplates.

Baptism, marriage, death or burial certificates.

Deeds concerning the freehold, leasehold or receipts for upkeep of graves.

Letters of past members, particularly from those abroad, and earlier than about 1850.

The name of the family lawyer, and any marriage settlements.

Old family portraits, miniatures, or photographs.

Medals and decorations, certificates of service in the Army, Navy or East India Company. Any family traditions of service in these forces, any particular regiments with which they have been connected.

Any family traditions of any sortwhatsoever, e.g. that they came from such and such a place or county, or from abroad, that they were engaged in a particular trade or occupation.

Specific Question
IDRIS GRYFFITH, when he died in 1876, was shown on his Death Certificate to be aged 74. This means, if accurate, he was born in 1801 or 1802 (according to whether he had had his birthday or not). Have you any information about where he was born, the names of his parents, whether he had any brothers or sisters, his occupation, where he lived during most of his lifetime, or any other information about him?

It appears, if married in England or Wales, he was married before July 1837. Have you any idea where and when he married, or the maiden name of his wife Gwyneth, or any other information about her?

APPENDIX B

Example of a Tabular Pedigree suitable for reproducing from typewriting and using only arabic figures.

Part of a pedigree of the family of EVANS OF HENBLAS

CHARLES EVANS of Trefeilir and Henblas, Llangefni, Anglesey (s. of William Evans of Trefeilir, High Sheriff 1733); High Sheriff 1752; m. Elizabeth, dau. of Hugh Lewis of Pont Newydd and had issue (with 3 sons & 2 daus. all of whom d.s.p.) a son,

HUGH EVANS, m. Elizabeth Rolt, dau. of James Furness, and grand-dau. of Sir Edward Baynton-Rolt Bt.; b. 1766, High Sheriff of Anglesey 1811, d. 20 Jny 1831, leaving issue (by her who d. 1856) a son,

CHARLES HENRY EVANS, of Trefeilir, Plasgwyn and Henblas, Co. Anglesey, m. 27 Jny 1832, Henrietta, dau. of the Very Rev. John Warren, Dean of Bangor, & d. 1 Nov 1855, having by her (who d. Jny 1889) had issue,

1. HENRY JOHN, b. 13 Feb 1833; d. 15 Jly 1855.
2. CHARLES HENRY, b. 16 Sept 1836; d. (from a wound received in the Crimea, while serving in the 55th Regt.) s.p. 4 Aug 1855.
3. WARREN EDWARD, now of Henblas.
4. ROWLAND HUGH, b. 19 Jny 1842; d. 19 Oct 1849.
5. MORGAN JOHN, b. 16 Jly 1845; m. 1st, 17 Jne 1875, Marie, dau. of Frederick James Beever, and by her has issue,

    (1) Constance Mabel.

    He m. 2ndly, Emily, dau. of John Owen, and has further issue,

    (1) Humphrey
    (2) Kenneth
    (3) Marjorie
    (4) Dorothy
    (5) Dulcibella.

1. HENRIETTA DULCIBELLA, b. 1834; m. 18 Oct 1859, Capt. John William Trevor, 55th Regt. A. de C.
2. CAROLINE MARIA, b. 1840; m. 7 Mch 1867, Rev. Canon T. W. Trevor, Rector of Llanfaely Tycroes, Anglesey, and has issue.
3. RHODA MARY, b. 1843: m. 21 Apr 1874, Lewes Golden, of Toowoomba, Queensland, and has issue.

APPENDIX C

SOME USEFUL ADDRESSES

ENGLAND

Army Museum Ogilvy Trust
Ministry of Defence (Army)
85 Whitehall
London SW1A 2NP

Army Records Centre
Bourne Avenue
Hayes, Middx UB3 1RS

Association of Genealogists and
Record Agents
Hon. Secretary
80 Pollard Road
London N20 0UD

Baptists Historical Society
Baptist Union Library
4 Southampton Row
London WC1B 4AB

British Library, Reference Division
Great Russell Street
London WC1B 3DG

British Red Cross Society
The Secretary
9 Grosvenor Crescent
London SW1X 7EI

Canterbury Cathedral Archives
and Library
The Precincts
Canterbury CT1 2EG

Catholic Central Library
47 Francis Street
London SW1P 1DN

Catholic Record Society
c/o Miss R. Rendel
114 Mount Street
London W1Y 6AH

Chaplain of the Fleet
Ministry of Defence
Lacon House
Theobalds Road
London WC1X 8RY

Church of Jesus Christ
of Latter Day Saints
Hyde Park Chapel
64 Exhibition Road
London SW7 2PA

Civil Service Department
Alencon Link
Basingstoke
Hants RG21 1 JB

College of Arms
Queen Victoria Street
London EC4V 4BT

Corporation of London
Record Office
Guildhall, London EC2P 2EJ

Federation of Family History Societies
General Secretary
96 Beaumont Street
Milehouse
Plymouth PL2 3AQ

General Register Office (CA Section)
Tichfield, Fareham, Hants PO15 5RU

General Register Office
Office of Population
Censuses and Surveys
St Catherine's House
10 Kingsway
London WC2B 6JP

General Registry
Finch Road
Douglas
Isle of Man

Greater London Record Office
County Hall
London SE1 7PB

Guildhall Library
Aldermanbury
London EC2P 2EJ

Historical Manuscripts Commission
Quality House, Quality Court
Chancery Lane, London WC2A 1HF

Home Office
Lunar House
40 Wellesley Road
Croydon CR9 2BY

Huguenot Library
University College
London WC1E 6BT

Huguenot Society
Miss I. Scouloudi, Hon. Secretary
67 Victoria Road
London W8 5RH

House of Lords Record Office
Westminster
London SW1

Imperial War Museum
(1914–18 War)
Lambeth Road
London SE1 6HZ

The Archivist
International Red Cross
British Red Cross Training Centre
Barnet Hill
Wonersh
Guildford
Surrey GU1 3PJ

India Office Library and Records
Foreign and Commonwealth Office
Orbit House
197 Blackfriars Road
London SE1 8NG

Irish Genealogical Society
of Great Britain
The Secretary
The Challoner Club
59–61 Pont Street
London SW1 0BD

Jewish Museum
Woburn House
Upper Woburn Place
London WC1H 0ED

John Rylands University Library
Oxford Road
Manchester M13 9PP

Lambeth Palace Library
London SE1 7JU

Land Registry
Lincoln's Inn Fields
London WC2A 3PH

Manx Museum Library
Kingswood Grove
Douglas
Isle of Man

National Army Museum
Royal Hospital Road
London SW3 4HT

National Maritime Museum
Greenwich
London SE10 9NF

Naval Personnel Records
(Recent records)
Room 2007 OS9 (a)
Ministry of Defence
Empress State Building
London SW6 1TR

Presbyterian Historical Society
of England
86 Tavistock Place
London WC1H 9RR

Principal Registry of the
Family Division (previously
Principal Probate Registry)
Somerset House
Strand, London WC2R 1LA

RAF Personnel Management Centre
Eastern Avenue
Barnwood
Gloucester GL4 7AN

Royal Artillery Record and
Manning Office
Imphal Barracks
York YO1 4HD

Royal Courts of Justice
Strand, London WC2A 2LL

Royal Marines Drafting and
Record Office
HMS *Centurion*
Grange Road
Portsmouth PO13 9XA

Salvation Army
(Investigating Officer for
tracing persons)
110-112 Middlesex Street
London E1 7HY

Society of Friends Library
Friends House, Euston Road
London NW1 2BJ

Society of Genealogists
14 Charterhouse Buildings
London EC1

Southampton City Record Office
Civic Centre
Southampton SO9 4XL

Spanish and Portuguese Synagogue
9 Lauderdale Road
Maida Vale
London W9 1LT

United Synagogue, Offices of the
Alder House, Woburn House
Upper Woburn Place
London WC1H 0ED

Dr. William's Library
14 Gordon Square
London WC1H 0AG
(Nonconformity generally)

The Weiner Library
4 Devonshire Street
London W1N 2BH

WALES

County Record Offices in Wales,
see Appendix D

The Hon. Society of Cymrodorion
118 Newgate Street
London EC1A 7AE

National Library of Wales
Aberystwyth, SY23 3BU

Registrar General of
Shipping and Seamen
Llantrisant Road
Llandaff
Cardiff CF5 2YS

University College of
North Wales Library
Department of Manuscripts
Bangor
Gwynedd LL57 2DG

University College of
Swansea Library
Singleton Park
Swansea SA2 8PP

Welsh Family History Societies
see Appendix E

SCOTLAND

National Library of Scotland
George IV Bridge
Edinburgh 1

Registrar General of Scotland
New Register House
Princes Street
Edinburgh EH1 3YT

Scots Ancestry Research Society
3 Albany Street
Edinburgh EH1 3PY

Scottish Genealogy Society
Miss Joan P. S. Ferguson
Honorary Secretary
21 Howard Place
Edinburgh EH3 5JY

Scottish Record Office
PO Box 36
HM General Register House
Edinburgh EH1 3YY

Scottish Tartans Society
Davidson House
Drummond Street
Comrie, Crieff
Perthshire

Court of the Lord Lyon
King of Arms
New Register House
Princes Street
Edinburgh EH1 3TY

NORTHERN IRELAND

Presbyterian Historical Society
of Northern Ireland
Church House
Fisherwick Place
Belfast BT1 6DU

Registrar General of Northern Ireland
Fermanagh House
Ormeau Avenue
Belfast BT2 8HX

Public Record Office of
Northern Ireland
66 Balmoral Avenue
Belfast BT9 6NY

General Register Office
Oxford House
49-55 Chichester Street
Belfast BT1 4HL

REPUBLIC OF IRELAND

Registrar General of Ireland
General Register Office
Custom House, Dublin 1

Public Record Office
Four Courts, Dublin 7

National Library of Ireland
Kildare Street, Dublin 2

Register of Deeds
Henrietta Street, Dublin

CHANNEL ISLANDS

The Registrar General
States Office
Royal Square, Jersey

Société Jersiaise
The Library
The Museum
9 Pier Road
Jersey

The Registrar General
The Greffe
St Peter Port
Guernsey

CANADA

British Columbia Genealogical Society
The Library
Langham College
100W 49th Avenue
Vancouver V5Y 2Z6
Canada

Maritime History Group
Memorial University of Newfoundland
St John's
Newfoundland
Canada

Public Archives of Canada
395 Wellington Street
Ottawa
Ontario K1A ON3
Canada

AUSTRALIA

Society of Australian Genealogists
Richmond Villa
120 Kent Street
Observatory Hill
Sydney NSW 2000

SOUTH AFRICA

Genealogical Society of South Africa
40 Haylett Street
Strand, Cape Town
South Africa

U.S.A.

British Information Service
845 Third Avenue
New York, NY 10022
U.S.A.

Genealogical Society of Utah
50 East North Temple
Salt Lake City
Utah 84150
U.S.A.

National Archives and Record Service
United States of America
General Services Administration
Washington DC 20408

APPENDIX D

COUNTY RECORD OFFICES IN WALES

Anglesey: *see* Gwynedd.

Caernarvonshire: *see* Gwynedd.

Cardiganshire: *see* Dyfed.

Carmarthenshire: *see* Dyfed.

Clwyd:

County Record Office, The Old Rectory, Hawarden, Deeside, Clwyd CH5 3NR. Telephone Hawarden 532364. Has public and official records from Flintshire, and a certain number of records from Denbighshire, held at 46 Clwyd Street, Ruthin, Clwyd LL15 1HP. Telephone Ruthin 3077.

Denbighshire: *see* Clwyd.

Dyfed:

Carmarthen Record Office, County Hall, Carmarthen SA31 1JP.

Pembrokeshire Record Office, The Castle, Haverfordwest.

Cardiganshire Record Office, Swyddfa'r Sir, Marine Parade, Aberystwyth, Dyfed.

Flintshire: *see* Clwyd.

Glamorgan:

Glamorgan Archive Service, County Hall, Cathays Park, Cardiff CF1 3NE. Contains archives accumulated by the former Cardiff City Library.

West Glamorgan Area Record Office, County Hall, Swansea SA1 3SN.

Gwent:

Gwent Record Office, County Hall, Cwmbran NP4 2XH. Holds records of former county of Monmouthshire.

Gwynedd:

Gwynedd Archives Service, Area Record Offices, Shirehall Street, Caernarfon, Gwynedd.

Main Archives for Gwynedd, including former county of Caernarfonshire.

Caernarfon Record Office, Victoria Dock, Caernarfon, Gwynedd.

Merionethshire: *see* Dyfed.

Monmouthshire: *see* Gwent; now forms part of Powys, q.v.

Pembrokeshire: *see* Dyfed.

Powys:

Powys Record Office, at present c/o Powys County Library, Llandrindod Wells.

Radnorshire: now part of Powys.

Dolgellau Record Office: Cae Penariag, Dolgellau, Gwynedd LL40 2YB.

Llangefni Record Office: Shire Hall, Llangefni, Gwynedd LL77 7TW. Branches at Caernarvon, Dolgellau and Llangefni.

APPENDIX E

FAMILY HISTORY SOCIETIES OF WALES

There are two main family history Directories, dealing with the whole of Wales. The first of these is:

The Association of Family Historians in Wales

This society, founded in March 1961, aims at promoting and co-ordinating the study of family history throughout Wales. Meeting twice a year, it makes representations to other bodies, including official bodies, on matters which affect Family History Societies in Wales, helping in the development of facilities which allow the societies to study family history, helping to make easy access to records helpful to them. It maintains a 'Register of Members' Interests for the whole of Wales' which it hopes to keep up-to-date. 2 Pen Lon, Menai Bridge, Gwynedd LL59 5LW.

The other body is the *Federation of Family History Societies* which maintains lists of its world-wide membership and publishes its 'Family History News and Digest' twice yearly, giving news of the activities of other societies and also publishes a number of low-priced booklets on aspects of research suitable for beginners and others. Full details of the Societies' addresses are available from the General Secretary. You are asked to enclose a stamped addressed envelope for the reply to your enquiry, or, if from abroad, two international postal reply coupons to the Secretary, 96 Beaumont Street, Milehouse, Plymouth PL3 5AQ.

The local family history societies are:

CLWYD FAMILY HISTORY SOCIETY, which covers Denbighshire, Flintshire, and a small part of Merioneth. 17 Parc-y-Llan, Llanfair Dyffryn Clwyd, Ruthin, Clwyd LL15 2YL.

DYFED FAMILY HISTORY SOCIETY, covering Cardiganshire, Carmarthenshire and Pembrokeshire. Pen-Llwyn-Howell, Alltwalis Road, Llanllawddog, Carmarthen, Dyfed SA32 7JF.

GWENT FAMILY HISTORY SOCIETY, covering Monmouthshire. 17 Craig Park Lane, Newport, Gwent NP4 6GX.

GWYNEDD FAMILY HISTORY SOCIETY, covering Anglesey, Caernarfonshire and the greater part of Merioneth. Glan Ffrwd, Pentreuchaf, Llanor, Pwllheli, Gwynedd LL53 8DJ.

POWYS FAMILY HISTORY SOCIETY, covering Breconshire, Montgomeryshire and Radnorshire. 34 Glebelands Road, Knutsford, Cheshire, WA16 9DZ.

SOUTH WALES FAMILY HISTORY SOCIETY, covering Glamorganshire and surrounding areas. 52 St Malo Road, Heath, Cardiff CF4 4HN.

BIBLIOGRAPHY

A SELECT BIBLIOGRAPHY FOR WALES

A Full Bibliography of genealogical books, many applicable also to Wales, will be found in the author's *In Search of Ancestry*, 4th edn. 1983.

HISTORY

DODD, A. H., *A Short History of Wales*, 1977

WILLIAMS, David, *A History of Modern Wales*, 2nd edn. 1977

WILLIAMS, William Retlaw, *The Parliamentary History of the Principality of Wales 1541–1895, comprising lists of Representatives, with biographical... notices of the members*, 1895.

NICHOLAS, Thomas, *Annals and Antiquities of the Counties and County Families of Wales*, 2nd edn., rev. and enlarged, 2 vols., 1875

BIOGRAPHY

Dictionary of National Biography, ed. by Sir Leslie Stephen and Sir Sidney Lee, published since 1917 by the Oxford University Press.

Dictionary of Welsh Biography (444–1940), 1959

HALL, Robert, *Welsh Local Records: details and classified topographical list.* Trans. of Hon. Cymmrodorion Soc., pp. 19–24, 1914

MEYRICK, Samuel Rush, *Heraldic Visitation of Wales and part of the Marches between the years 1586 and 1611*, 2 vols., 1946 (from the MS of Lewis Dwnn)

GENERAL GUIDES

BARROW, Geoffrey B., *The Genealogist's Guide*, 1977. [This up-dates Marshall and Whitmore]

CAMP, Anthony John, *Everyone has Roots*, 1978

A Guide to Genealogical Sources in the National Library of Wales, Nat. Library of Wales Pamphlet

HAMILTON-EDWARDS, Gerald K. S., *In Search of Ancestry*, 4th edn., 1983

Handlist of Scottish and Welsh Publications . . . Welsh Section by Idred Lewes, British Record. Assoc. Publications, Pamphlet No. 4, 1954

JONES, Francis, 'An Approach to Welsh Genealogy', *Transactions of the Hon. Soc. of Cymmrodorion* (Session 1948), 1949

MATTHEWS, Constance Mary, *Your Family History*, 2nd edn., 1983

MARSHALL, George William, *Genealogist's Guide*, 1903 (last edn., 1953)

STEEL, Donald John, *Discovering Your Family History*, 1980

THOMSON, Theodore Radford, *A Catalogue of British Family Histories*, 2nd edn., 1935

WAGNER, Sir Anthony, *English Genealogy*, 3rd edn., 1983

WAGNER, Sir Anthony, *English Ancestry*, 1961 [a shortened form of the above]

WELSH CHRISTIAN NAMES AND SURNAMES

MORGAN, Prys, Chapter 2, 'Welsh Surnames' in *Background to Wales: a course of studies in modern Welsh life*, 1968

MORGAN, T. J. and MORGAN, Prys, *Welsh Surnames*, University of Wales Press, 1985 [a recently published, valuable and scholarly work]

REANEY, Percy Hide, *A Dictionary of British Surnames*, 2nd edn., 1976, rev. by R. M. Wilson [contains a useful section on Welsh surnames]

WITHYCOMBE, Elizabeth Gidley, *The Oxford Dictionary of English Christian Names*, 3rd edn., 1977

CIVIL AND PARISH REGISTERS

CHURCH of Jesus Christ of Latter Day Saints, Parish and Vital Records. Apply Deseret Enterprises Ltd., Manchester Distribution Centre, 18 Hammond Avenue, White Hill Industrial Estate, Stockport, Cheshire. Lists of all records (including the International Genealogical Index (I.G.I.)) covered by the C.F.I. at date of publication

REGISTRAR GENERAL, *List of Non-Parochial Registers and Records in the Custody of the Registrar General of Births, Deaths and Marriages, 1841*, 1859

SOCIETY OF GENEALOGISTS, *Catalogue of Parish Register Copies*. 1. Those held in the Society; 2. Those held elsewhere.

WILLS AND ADMINISTRATIONS

CAMP, Anthony John, *Wills and their Whereabouts*, 1974. [The introduction gives an excellent account of the history, development, custom and form of wills from earliest times in Great Britain, giving full details of the various courts throughout their history]

GIBSON, Jeremy S. W., *Wills and Where to Find Them*, 1974

GIBSON, Jeremy S. W., *A Simple Guide to Probate Jurisdictions*, 1980 (contains maps of Wales jurisdictions]

NONCONFORMISTS IN WALES

STEEL, Donald John, vol. 2 of the *National Index of Parish Registers* (1972) covers in detail all Nonconformist Denominations

MONUMENTAL INSCRIPTIONS

WHITE, Henry Leslie, *Monuments and their Inscriptions*, 1978

TOPOGRAPHY

HUMPHERY-SMITH, Cecil (ed.), *Phillimore Atlas and Index of Parish Registers* [Welsh section in 4 maps can be obtained separately from Phillimore & Co.]

LEWIS, Samuel, *Topographical Dictionary of Wales*, 2 vols., 4th edn., 1845

DEEDS AND DOCUMENTS in National Library of Wales

GREEN, Francis, Editor of *West Wales Historical Records*, Aberystwyth, 1921. [This is unindexed but gives an indication of the many and varied types of deeds to be found among the MSS. of this great library]

JOURNALS

British Association for Local History, *The Local Historian* [qtly]

Federation of Family History Societies, *Family History, News and Digest*

SOCIETY OF GENEALOGISTS, *Genealogists' Magazine* [qtly]

ARMY

FORTESCUE, Sir John William, *A History of the British Army*, 13 vols. with 6 atlases, 1899-1920

HAMILTON-EDWARDS, Gerald K. S., *In Search of Army Ancestry* 1927

WHITE, Arthur S., *A Bibliography of Regimental Histories of the British Army*, 1965

NAVY

CLOWES, Sir William Laird, *The Royal Navy: a history from the earliest times to to the present*, 7 vols., 1897-1903

LEWIS, Michael Arthur, *The Navy of Britain*, 1948

LEWIS, Michael Arthur, *The Navy in Transition, 1814–1864, a social history*, 1965

LEWIS, Michael Arthur, *A Social History of the Navy 1793–1815*, 1960

MERCHANT SERVICE

COX, Nicholas, 'The Records of the Registrar-General of Shipping and Seamen' (account published in the journal *Sources for Maritime History*, vol. 2, no. 2 (Sept., 1972)).
There is also a 5-page leaflet 'Records of the Registrar General of Shipping and Seamen' issued by the Public Record Office in 1973

EAST INDIA COMPANY

FOSTER, Sir William, *Guide to the India Office Records, 1600–1858*, 1919, repr. 1966

LANCASTER, Joan C., 'The India Office Records: a brief description', *Archives*, vol. 9, no. 43 (April 1970).

NEWSPAPERS

The Times Tercentenary Handlist of English and Welsh Newspapers and Reviews 1620–1920, 1920

MANOR COURT AND CHANCERY RECORDS

GARRET, Robert Edmund Francis, *Chancery and Other Legal Proceedings*, 1968

HONE, N. J., *The Manor and Manorial Records*, 1925

RETURNS OF OWNERS OF LAND of one acre and upwards . . . England and Wales, 2 vols, 1875

WEST, John, *Village Records*, 2nd edn., Phillimore, 1982

HERALDRY

BOUTELL, Charles, *Boutell's Heraldry*, rev. by J. P. Brooke-Little, 1978

CHESSHYRE, D. H. B., *The Identification of Coats of Arms on British Silver*, 1978

FAIRBAIRN, James, *Fairbairn's Crests of the Families of Great Britain and Ireland . . . rev. by Laurence Butters.* 1968 [originally published in 2 vols.]

FOX-DAVIES, Arthur Charles, *A Complete Guide to Heraldry*, rev. and annotated by J. P. Brooke-Little, 1968. [Still the best general work on English Heraldry]

MEYRICK, Samuel Rush, *Heraldic Visitation of Wales and part of the Marches between the years 1586 and 1613*, 2 vols., 1846. [From the MS. of Lewis Dwnn]

MONCRIEFFE OF THAT ILK, Sir Rupert Iain Kay, Bart., and POTTINGER, Don, *Simple Heraldry, cheerfully illustrated*, 1953. [Amusingly written and illustrated and at the same time full of sound accurate information]

SCOTT-GILES, Charles Wilfred, *The Romance of Heraldry*, 1951

SQUIBB, George Drewey, *Visitation Pedigrees and the Genealogist*, 2nd edn., 1978

WAGNER, Sir Anthony Richard, *Heralds of England: a history of the Office and College of Arms*, 1967

INDEX

Abbreviations:

NLW	National Library of Wales
PRO	Public Record Off, London
PRO, Kew	Public Record Office, Kew